by the sea

Robin Jones Gunn

HARVEST HOUSE PUBLISHERS
EUGENE, OREGON

W0006227

Published in association with Books & Such Literary Management, www.booksandsuch.com.

Cover and interior design by Studio Gearbox.
All photo credits are on page 175.

This logo is a federally registered trademark of the Hawkins Children's LLC. Harvest House Publishers, Inc., is the exclusive licensee of this trademark.

By the Sea
Copyright © 2025 by Robin's Nest Productions, Inc.
Published by Harvest House Publishers
Eugene, Oregon 97408
www.harvesthousepublishers.com

ISBN 978-0-7369-9038-7 (hardcover)
ISBN 978-0-7369-9039-4 (eBook)

Library of Congress Control Number: 2024942258

Printed in China

25 26 27 28 29 30 31 32 33 / LP / 10 9 8 7 6 5 4 3 2 1

For my favorite surfer boys,

who are the most treasured men in my life:

my dad, my husband, my son, and my three grandsons.

I love the ocean even more because of

the way all six of you showed me

how to frolic by the sea.

contents

Sandy Toes: Sunny Days at the Shore

Sonnets for the Sea.. 11

Going and Coming... 15

Near the Sea... 17

Morning Clouds on a Summer Day.................................... 20

The Sea Hath Its Pearls... 23

Coastal View... 29

Sunset at San Clemente... 31

The Fellowship of the Firepit 37

Friends and Fog.. 41

The Gift... 47

Remember Me 49

Get Your Vitamin Sea.. 55

Known... 59

Deep Blue: Mysteries of the Vast Ocean

Under the Sea 69

Here Be Dragons 79

Dutch Masters 85

The Red Sea and Me 88

Symphony of the Sea 91

After the Rain 97

Heavens to Betsey 99

Peace Be Still 109

Sea Sonnet 117

Island Dreams: Tropical Bliss

Hololani 121

Home of My Heart 125

Trade Winds 126

Fifty-Two Saturdays by the Sea 131

Your Love 135

Dolphins 137

Island Sand 143

Beach Wedding 149

On the Fifth Day 150

Akamai Island Breeze 152

Tommy the Turtle 157

Breakfast on the Beach 165

Could It Be Today? 171

Notes 173

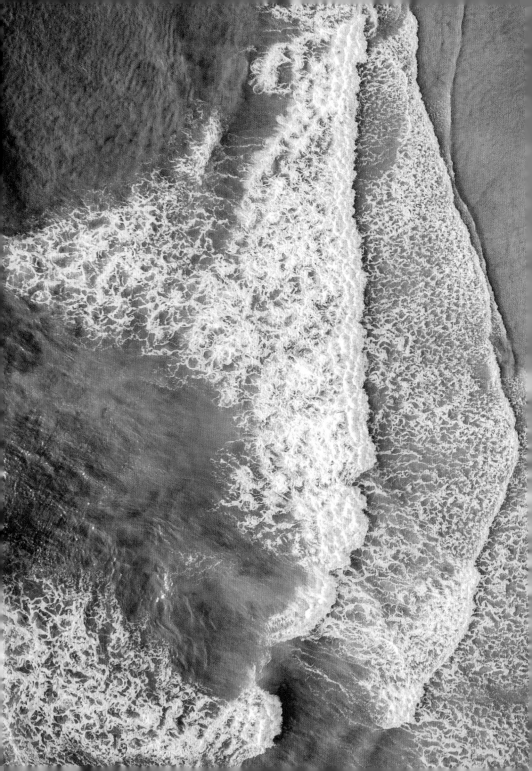

sandy toes

sunny days at the shore

God called the dry ground "land," and the gathered
waters he called "seas." And God saw that it was good.

Genesis 1:10

sonnets for the sea

Do you remember your first visit to the sea?

Mine was a family trek to Newport Beach. I was almost five years old. We had just moved from Wisconsin to Southern California. I remember running to the water's edge, slipping out of my sneakers, and testing the cool sand with my bare feet. Unfurling before me was the vast Pacific Ocean with all its salty fragrance and rhythmic sound of the waves as they slid to the shore and curled back to the sea.

My brother, sister, and I dug for buried treasure and collected tiny shells. The golden afternoon felt frozen in time as we ran and laughed and then returned to the blanket where Mom handed us peanut butter sandwiches seasoned with a few granules of sand. Brazen seagulls made broad-winged swooping attempts to snatch our lunch out of our hands. Dad kept saying that, if we were back "home," he would be shoveling snow.

The afternoon sun sauntered toward the horizon, leaving a silver trail in her wake. Our shadows stretched out long across the wet sand, and Dad announced it was time to go, but that we would be back soon.

I have a black-and-white photo my mom took of us that day. You can't make out our faces, but our poses give away our sense of newness and simple joy. Rolled-up pant legs, my sister with her hands on hips, my dad looking as if he had conquered a new land. Our posture says, "We are beach people now. We belong here."

My love of the sea began that day and it has remained a true love. Over the years, many of my happiest vacations have been spent at various beaches on this beautiful planet.

Perhaps the same is true for you. You hold close the many memories made with family and friends under beach umbrellas or sailing across the blue. You still have the small shells you found while strolling along a shoreline laced with white squiggles of sea froth.

Every visit to the sea is different, isn't it? The tides change, the winds shift, clouds gather and flee. Sunsets never grow old. The invitation to come as we are is always open. After every visit we leave a little changed too. The burdens of our hearts don't feel quite so heavy. Gloomy thoughts have cleared our minds. We can breathe again. Fresh dreams rise to the surface, and we are renewed.

If you're holding this book, you likely are a fellow lover of the sea. You are well acquainted with the way the ocean nourishes something burrowed inside you that hibernates when routines take command of your life. You need to hear the song of the waves, which can echo in your thoughts on dark nights. You have experienced the way the sunshine can quench an inner thirst like nothing else.

Some of the times you've found yourself lost in prayer or most deeply in awe of God likely were moments when your toes were anchored in the cool sand. You know how a stroll on a pristine stretch of beach can settle your windswept soul.

This book is for all of us who love the sand, the sun, and all that comes with the joy of being near the ocean. It is my sonnet for the sea, composed with affection. As you turn these pages, my wish is that the lovely images and heartfelt words will kindle memories of moments that you've savored being by the sea. May you catch glimpses of eternity and see reflections in your own life of the gift of simple hope.

THE SEA! the sea! the open sea!
The blue, the fresh, the ever free.

       Bryan Waller Procter

going and coming

Norman Rockwell's side-by-side painting entitled *Going and Coming* reminds me of childhood trips to the beach. The famous Americana artist painted two images of the same family. In the morning scene, they are full of vigor as they head off with a small rowboat strapped to the car's roof. The tandem image then shows them on their way home at dusk, rosy cheeked and subdued. Mom is asleep, and Dad looks as if he can barely keep his eyes open.

I'm sure that, during my childhood, my family looked much the same on our eagerly anticipated jaunts to the sea.

On those wonderful "let's go to the beach" mornings, I recall Mom packing snacks in a red metal cooler and the unmistakable scent of the Coppertone sun lotion she slathered on our fair skin. I remember my dad whistling as he loaded the station wagon, and I loved the feel of the wind through the rolled-down windows as we took off down the street.

Our drive home, I'm sure, mirrored the droopy-eyed models in Rockwell's painting. Sand in our hair, a swath of sunburn

Please, oh please
May we go to the sea?
Today I want to be
Wild and free.

RJG

across our noses, big yawns, and a bucket of tiny seashells in my sister's lap.

For us, the beach of choice was Corona del Mar. Since we weren't the only ones who decided it was the best beach for a family outing, we would try to arrive midmorning and lug our gear down to the shore to stake our patch of sand for the day. We didn't set up camp the way some folks did. Those families arrived with a fleet of beach chairs and colorful umbrellas that popped upward like a California poppy when the afternoon breeze kicked up. The kids in those families brought loads of toys and water floaties to keep them occupied.

For my sister and me, our entertainment started with burying our little brother in the sand so that only his head was showing. He eventually would break free, and the three of us would spend hours scooping up skittering sand crabs and creating sandcastles with moats. Then we would stand back when the big waves came in and wait for the saltwater to fill the moats while hopefully leaving our castles still standing.

Our favorite shoreline activity was gathering up ropes of bulbous, dried seaweed and popping the pods. Some pods still had water in them, and we would explode in riotous laughter at the rude sounds they could make.

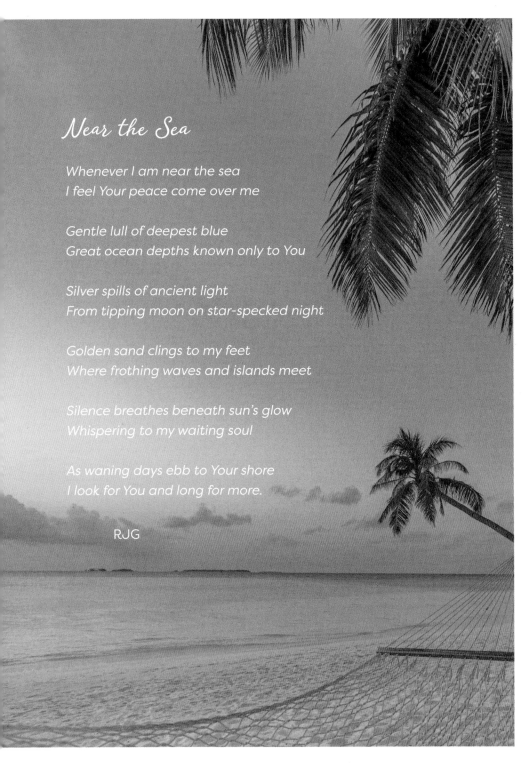

Near the Sea

Whenever I am near the sea
I feel Your peace come over me

Gentle lull of deepest blue
Great ocean depths known only to You

Silver spills of ancient light
From tipping moon on star-specked night

Golden sand clings to my feet
Where frothing waves and islands meet

Silence breathes beneath sun's glow
Whispering to my waiting soul

As waning days ebb to Your shore
I look for You and long for more.

RJG

Mom stayed in her beach chair, with the tails of her headscarf fluttering. Through her cat-eye sunglasses she kept track of our seaside shenanigans. Our dad, ever the athlete, loved the water. He would spend hours diving under the swells and going beyond the surf to swim laps parallel to the shore.

When the waves were just right, his aquatic interests would shift, and I'd stop building sandcastles to watch him. My hero. As a wave began to crest, he would position himself carefully, glance over his shoulder, and start swimming with his face fixed on the shore. His straightened frame would blend with the unfurling wave, and I'd observe, mesmerized, the way he bodysurfed to shore as effortlessly as if he were a dolphin.

Then one summer day I felt I was old enough to stop being a spectator. I asked my dad to teach me how to ride the waves the way he did. The camaraderie he had with the ocean lured me past the knee-deep water. I wanted to make friends with the surf the way my father had.

I was a slow learner, and undoubtedly I shed an excess of tears. I wasn't an athletic child, nor was I very coordinated. Those factors didn't seem to matter to the waves, because at last, the moment came when I got it right. The exhilaration of being lifted by foaming seawater and powerfully carried all the way to the shore was unforgettable. I felt as if I had politely reached out to shake hands with the wild sea, and in its untamed exuberance, the ocean had scooped me up and enfolded me in a hug. We were now forever friends.

That night, when I turned my head, saltwater trickled from my ear and dampened my pillow. If I lay completely still and closed my eyes, I could feel the movement of the water as if my body were still rising and falling with the waves.

I understood why true watermen and women carry their heavy surfboards through the sand and paddle out even on stormy days. No wonder an entire industry has been built on surfboards and boogie boards, leashes, wet suits, and the right kind of fins for bodysurfers. There's nothing like having a curling, foaming wave lift you like a javelin and propel you forward rather than slamming you down or turning you around in an underwater somersault.

I was smitten.

Years later, on my first date with the man who became my husband, I asked if he had any hobbies or played any sports.

He smiled and said he loved to bodysurf.

I think that was the moment I knew he and I would become the next generation to reenact together the Rockwell-style "going and coming" summer days at the beach.

Exultation is the going
    Of an inland soul to sea —
Past the houses, past the headlands,
    Into deep Eternity!

Emily Dickinson

Morning Clouds on a Summer Day

Morning clouds
glide on unseen breath
pure white wishes
set adrift in an
unblemished sky

Slowly floating
suddenly changing
steadily moving on

My heart calls out
to the kindred clouds
my spirit glides beside them
blown by an unseen breath.

All my wishes, all my hopes,
my yet-to-be-imagined dreams
are ever adrift
ever shifting in shape and size.

And on they go
Where they go,
their destination determined
by the One
who breathes life over me

Breathe on me
oh breath of God
guide my whimsy-filled heart
direct my wayward wishes.

RJG

the sea hath its pearls

In my early days as a writer, I was looking around one of those funny-smelling secondhand shops when I spotted a print in a lovely gold frame. I made my way toward the image of the Victorian woman captured in the painting as if we were at a crowded, noisy party, but she was the person I wanted to meet.

She stood on a shoreline, where pastel blue waters gently receded, examining a small treasure in the palm of her hand. Her auburn hair was twisted in a windblown chignon, and her other hand lifted her flowing ivory frock from the water's edge, uncovering her toes. Only her profile was revealed in the painting. She was caught up in the wonder of her discovery.

I bought the captivating picture and hung it in my cozy writing room. For many years my unnamed friend spoke to me of the beauty of the shore, of taking time to pause and marvel at even the smallest gifts tucked away in creation.

One day I made a small discovery about the picture. Upon closer inspection, I noticed that what she held in her open hand looked like a sand-covered pearl. On discovering the reason for her focused awe, my imagination amplified what that experience would be like.

Envision strolling along the beach and finding a real pearl washed onto the shore. What momentous action could have caused the oyster to release its gift? For months or even years, the oyster had adjusted to whatever invasive irritant embedded itself in its tender core. Rather than causing permanent damage to the heart of the oyster, the unwanted invader had been transformed. It had been smoothed and changed into a highly valued gift of beauty.

The picture spoke to me deeply and personally that day. An unwanted, invasive challenge had become embedded at the core of my vulnerable heart. I needed to know that somehow a small treasure could be formed in me in spite of, or possibly because of, the pain. I wanted to believe that God could smooth and transform the hurtful experience into something of value.

Faithfully, the Creator's gentle ways did their healing work over the months and years that followed. The day came when my posture, like that of the woman on the shore, was to bow my head and gaze in wonder at the treasure I now held in the palm of my life. A precious gift, formed in the darkness.

The years rolled on, like faithful tides. I wrote many books in the company of my graceful beachcomber friend, fixed as she was on the wall. She became the best sort of companion for my novelist's imagination. There she was, encapsulated in her own world and charmed within her own moment. I worked beside her, dreaming up characters who stood on the shore of their lives, struggling with their own conundrums of unwanted irritants, and eventually discovering they, too, had been given treasures formed in the darkness.

Exiled

Searching my heart for its true sorrow,
This is the thing I find to be:
That I am weary of words and people,
Sick of the city, wanting the sea;

Wanting the sticky, salty sweetness
Of the strong wind and shattered spray;
Wanting the loud sound and the soft sound
Of the big surf that breaks all day.

Edna St. Vincent Millay

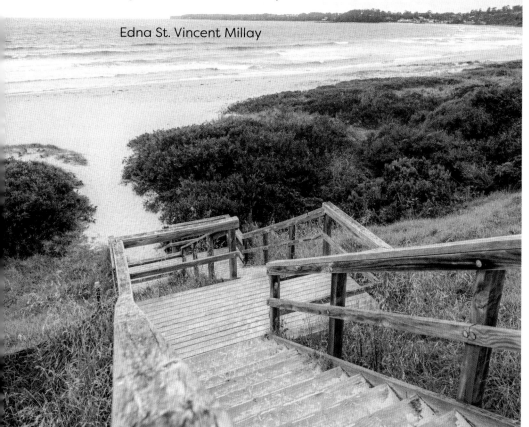

An unexpected adventure took my husband and me to Sydney, Australia. We arrived in the early afternoon, dazed after the eighteen-hour flight. The following day held a radio interview and a meeting with Australian book distributors. We decided to use the remaining daylight hours in our new down-under time zone to take a walk and hope that would help us sleep that night.

At the end of a lovely green trail, we came upon the impressive entrance of the Art Gallery of New South Wales. Surprisingly, admission was free, so we went inside, hand in hand, admiring the beautiful collections. We meandered our way to the south building and both stopped simultaneously, mouths agape.

She was there!

In golden glory, the nearly life-sized original painting of my quiet muse and longtime companion was on display right where she had been since she was painted in England by William Henry Margetson in 1897.

I approached her as if I were meeting a pen pal for the first time. The details were remarkable in the oil painting on the large canvas. I studied her bare toes in the tawny sand, the upswept folds of her gown embroidered in blue with a matching sash, and loved the way her skirt-clutching hand was pressed to her heart. Tears formed as I studied the luminous painting. What a beautiful, more complete story she was able to tell in oil paint than in the faded reproduction I had spotted in the back of a this-and-that shop so long ago.

I never had known who her artist was, nor had I searched to find the title given to the painting. On the plaque beneath her on the wall read *The Sea Hath Its Pearls*.

I pressed my hand to my heart and whispered, "Yes. Yes, it does."

A Seaside Walk

We walked beside the sea
After a day which perished silently
Of its own glory...

The sky above us showed
A universal and unmoving cloud
On which the cliffs permitted us to see
Only the outline of their majesty...

And shining with gloom, the water gray
Swang in its moon-taught way.

Elizabeth Barrett Browning

coastal view

"Ah, a slice of blue, a coastal view. Yes, please."

I scribbled those words across the top of a fresh page in my journal early on a June morning. Twenty minutes earlier I had boarded a train in Old Town San Diego. After helping myself to a cup of English breakfast tea, I settled in on the west side of the train, eager to gaze at the ocean on my five-hour trek north to Ventura. The day before, I'd spoken at a university in San Diego and knew I couldn't fly home to Maui without going to see the special treasure that awaited me at the end of the line—our daughter, her husband, and their three-year-old son.

Baby Blue, as I had called him from the day he was born, loved trains. He had watched the Amtrak Pacific Surfliner many times when it pulled into the station located by the beach. Big, loud trains were something not found on Maui where he was born. They had become one of the new and fun parts of his world now that their family had moved to California.

Much had changed in his young life, and I wondered if he would know me when I arrived. It had been seven months since

I'd given him a cuddle and heard him call me by my Hawaiian nickname for grandma, Tutu. I couldn't wait to scoop him up and start making new memories.

I leaned back and looked out the window as the coastal fog lifted and a slice of blue came into focus. Soon I was staring at a full, expansive view of the white-capped Pacific Ocean as it stretched all the way to the horizon. This was exactly the vista I had wished for. A slice of blue. The unforgettable California coastal view, which I hadn't gazed at for many years.

As the train rolled on past the lifeguard station near the pier at San Clemente, I smiled. It looked just as I had remembered it from years ago. When I was in grade school, every Fourth of July our family stayed overnight with friends who had a beachfront house not far from that particular lifeguard stand. The best sort of childhood memories happened on that beach with laughter-filled afternoons bobbing in the waves and soaking up our vitamin D. In the evening, as soon as the sun melted into the sea, we made s'mores, watched Roman candles being shot off the pier, and danced in the sand with twirling sparklers in both hands.

The train stopped to pick up more passengers before we continued north. I thought of how many times I'd been to the various beaches we were passing. During my teen years, going to the beach was a regular social event. Very early on some Saturday mornings, a friend down the street picked me up in his VW van with his surfboard strapped to the roof. We would make a couple of stops to pick up more friends before buying doughnuts in Laguna Beach and then scooting down the Pacific Coast Highway to his favorite surf spot.

Sunset at San Clemente

The sun
A perfect orange,
enormous and ripe
sinks until it is sliced in half
at the edge of the world

Silently it slides
juice, rind, and all
over the blue cliff
into the unknown tomorrow

RJG

> Live in the sunshine, swim the sea,
> drink the wild air's salubrity.
>
> Ralph Waldo Emerson

Dawn Patrol, the surfers called it. They would pull on their wet suits, paddle through the water, occasionally catch a wave here and there, and talk about us girls. At least, we wanted to think they were talking about us.

My girlfriends and I would huddle close, with shared Mexican blankets around our shoulders. We always talked about the guys. We knew who liked whom and who was really cool. We also knew, deep down, that we were the groupies. The beach girls who were always willing to help with gas money to ensure future Saturday morning invitations to go out with the surfers on Dawn Patrol. These guys would take us to the beach but never to the prom.

That was okay because the guys we really liked were the ones in the youth group at our large church. Those guys were the ones who brought wood for the firepits at Newport Beach on a Saturday night. One of them always brought a guitar. As the stars came out, my girlfriends and I would smile at them through the rising amber flames. We would straighten wire coat hangers to roast marshmallows and sing familiar choruses back when it was still cool to spontaneously sing around a campfire. Those nights hope sprouted, and my girlfriends and I went home to dream about marrying one of those hoodie-wearing guys someday.

My dream came true. I married one of those guys.

Thinking of my husband, as the train churned up the miles, going farther north, made me wish he had come with me on this trip. He would have his own album of childhood and high school beach memories that would come in focus on this train. Our shared beach memories began when we dated in our twenties. Jumping in his sports car and heading up Highway 1 became our favorite kind of date, even after we were married. I thought about how you can feel a fresh sort of freedom in your bones when you speed along in a convertible with the ocean in view. The only thing you need to do is draw in one deep draft of sea air after another.

Those were the days.

The closer the train came to Ventura, the more the Pacific Ocean came back into view. By then, the early afternoon sun had warmed the colors to a rich shade of indigo and scattered a line of bright light along the crest of the waves. I felt so young, drinking in the sight.

Truth was, I no longer wore an embroidered gauze shirt or folded my long hair into a braid. I wasn't strolling along the shore at Newport Beach or practicing cartwheels with my childhood pals at San Clemente. I was a grandma. In a few minutes, I would shake off all the sweet memories, step off this train, and reenter the season of life I was delighting in now.

A blue-eyed three-year-old would be waiting on the platform.

The Ventura station was announced, and the train came to a stop. I headed to the exit and leaned to look out the window. There he was! Standing alert, holding his mom's hand, fascinated by the train. The breeze off the ocean tousled his wavy blond hair. His eyes were wide, watching the uniformed conductor who took my suitcase and placed it on the platform.

I drew in a deep sniff of the familiar, slightly fishy scent of the ocean air and tried to squelch my nervous flutters. What if my grandson didn't remember me? He couldn't possibly remember all the stories I'd read to him or the many Maui afternoons when he had splashed in the wading pool in our backyard. Who would he think I was when I wanted to wrap my arms around him?

I stepped off the train and took one step toward him, then another, holding my breath.

"Tutu! Tutu! It's Tutu!" His small voice echoed over the rumble of the train.

Breaking from his mom, my island boy ran to me, yelling, "Tutu! It's you! On a train!"

He was in my arms, squeezing me as my heart rose like an ocean swell.

He knew me.

He came to me.

I was no longer the vague memory of a lady who lived in the little yellow house so very far away. I was his one and only Tutu who came to him from across the sea and miraculously emerged from a train.

Wherever I cause my name to be remembered ...I will come to you and bless you.

Exodus 20:24 NLT

the fellowship of the firepit

Something happens around a glowing beach firepit that doesn't happen anywhere else in life. I don't feel the same closeness with companions seated on benches around campfires in the mountains, as enjoyable as that is. Gaslit backyard firepits surrounded by Adirondack chairs are inviting and have provided some memorable moments, but it's not the same.

At the beach, the surroundings set the tone. When I nestle in a pocket of sand, still warm from the day, I feel drawn close to friends and family in an elemental way. We are being touched by earth, wind, and fire. We're as close as we can be to those fundamentals of nature. The beach has emptied of its daytime devotees, and now it's us. Just us.

For our clan, summer nights around a campfire at the beach marked the belly button of the year. In the scope of an entire year, with all its variations, those moments were right in the center of the calendar and formed my favorite of all the seasons.

After our little ones spent the afternoon frolicking in the surf and sand, we would gather close and watch the horizon. The

sun, like a big sugar cookie, would dunk into the wide rim of the ocean's cup. There it would dissolve as invisible fingers made pink icing streaks across the primrose sky.

"God is finger painting again," my husband would say.

The stars would appear one by one like crumbs across a table-cloth. In the deepening of the night, we felt the cool breath of the misty ocean breeze and heard the rising crash of the tide.

Comfort came from the crackling sound of the wood as it caught fire. The warmth rising from the yellow flames toasted the front of us while we drew close and wrapped our dried beach towels around us to warm our backsides. Sparks rose into the air, carrying our hushed words with them and turning the eventide into hal-lowed time.

And in this fellowship we enjoy
the eternal life He promised us.

I John 2:25 NLT

Those were the hours of roasted hot dogs and gooey marsh-mallows. The moments when we drew close. Close enough so I could cuddle my busy little girl in my lap and draw in the scent of the baked-in saltwater on her skin. Close enough to talk or sing or say nothing at all. Close enough to laugh and for me to reshape thoughts of all the wearying days of motherhood into feelings of privilege and simple joy.

In the same way that those golden sunsets and smoky camp-fires were a feast for our eyes and ears, the fellowship of the firepit was a feast for my heart.

friends and fog

My friend was only a quarter of a century into her interesting life when we met in England. I was a bit older. Two women of words. As is the peculiar way of friendship, we tilted our heads like birds of a feather and knew we would meet again someday, somewhere, for Part Two of our conversation.

Since then, we've seen each other a dozen times over the past few decades, and every visit is a comfortable continuation of our first chat. We've been to each other's homes, which is remarkable because we live an ocean apart. At one time, we lived two oceans apart. She came to visit me when I lived in Hawaii and experienced her first snorkel cruise. A few years later I crossed the two oceans between us and arrived on her doorstep with jet lag. Her solution was to take me on a safari.

When a business trip recently brought her to California, where my husband and I had just moved, she and I decided we needed a small adventure, so we rented a bungalow at Newport Beach. The cottage came complete with a Dutch door and shutters that had

> For whatever we lose (like a you or a me)
> it's always ourselves we find in the sea.
>
> E.E. Cummings

carved-out designs in the wood. Our two-night slumber party included lots of tea, an assortment of cookies, and many stories.

On our first morning, the sunshine beckoned us outside to walk to the beach, only four blocks away. Being women who required little, we took off in our flip-flops, summer dresses with sweaters, and the key to the cottage in my pocket. I said something about us being cute beachy women of leisure for the day.

Very few people were on the beach that November morning. We watched some surfers in wet suits, a couple walking their dog, and a guy in lifeguard-red shorts jogging by, his bare feet leaving the only footprints that day along the shoreline.

The view of perfectly blended blue on blue invited us to sit in the sand and stretch out our legs. The beauty silenced us. Both of us had trusted God with our hearts and souls at an early age. Both of us had known pain, loss, fear, and heartache. And both of us had known the favor of the Lord with our endeavors. We were rich in experiences and had traveled this wide world.

We had nothing to prove. Nothing to process.

We were content to simply be in a *selah* moment. Selah—the ancient term that invites us to pause and ponder—is a valuable observation for any age. Thoughts shift and souls become quiet worshippers in the invisible cathedral that encloses us.

I realized, in that sacred place on the beach, that it had been a long time since I had given space in my schedule for this life-giving practice of pausing and pondering. I lived close enough to drive down to the beach every day, but months had passed since I'd last gone to the beach for the afternoon. I was forgetting how to sit, alone or with a friend, and just be.

This oversight had a remedy. I could take time to nurture my weary heart, mind, and body. It took doing so with my friend to recognize the cavity in my brimming schedule. The hollow place in my spirit could be filled.

I don't know what sort of ponderings occupied my companion's thoughts during our long gaze at the endless sea. I knew she would tell me if she wanted to talk about it. I was grateful for this moment.

The horizon seemed to cloud over in the distance, and I blinked, thinking my eyes had dried out from the cool air. No, it wasn't my eyesight blurring. It was the air around us. Everything was turning hazy. A determined wall of fog came our way like a steamroller, flattening the waves as it steadily moved toward the beach.

We had been sitting without moving for quite a while, and I discovered my legs had turned to jelly. My first attempts to pop up to a standing position were unsuccessful. Plopping in the sand when we first arrived had felt so carefree. We weren't the sort who needed folding beach chairs. Or were we?

The limber frames that once housed our souls when we first met were now twice as old. While another quarter of a century had filled our lives with beautiful experiences, it had also turned our bodies into uncooperative frenemies. I attempted to stand again and found I was only moving the shifting sand around underneath me.

Look at that sea, girls—
    all silver and shadow and vision of
    things not seen.
We couldn't enjoy its loveliness any
    more if we had millions of dollars
    and ropes of diamonds.
    Lucy Maud Montgomery

The fog was past the end of the jetty, and we knew we would soon be covered with the thick white mist. A socked-in foggy beach would limit our sight and make it harder to find our way across the wide stretch of sand back to our abode.

When I tried to get up again, I rolled to my side and rose to my knees. My long dress became tangled, and I couldn't complete the next step of balancing on one leg without either tearing the dress or tipping myself over onto my side. All I could do was laugh.

To my pal's credit, she had withheld her laughter until that moment. When she saw me on all fours, tugging at the excessive fabric and slapping my numb leg trying to convince it to cooperate, she burst into laughter. I kept giggling, too, and flopped belly-down in the sand.

The encroaching fog rolled over us as we made hilarious efforts to bolster each other up and get on our feet. We did it. And managed to find our flip-flops in the strange condensation that now covered us. Hurrying to reach the sidewalk, we laughed as we stumbled, along with the misty creature from the deep on our heels.

Thankfully, in all the tumbling the key to the bungalow hadn't slipped out of my pocket. We retreated into the warm cottage and lit the vintage stove. Time to put on the kettle. Now, where did we put those cookies?

Some friends simply weather the many seasons of life with you better than others. If you ever want to know who those friends are, put on your flowing maxi dress and take them to a California beach on such a winter's day.

The Gift

Gentle evening breeze
smooths the surface of the sea
turning the water
to tissue-paper lavender blue

"Today has been a gift,"
I say.

The sky agrees and sends
Wispy pink clouds
to spread their silken ribbons
across the sea
and entwine them around me.

RJG

remember me

Some of my favorite people are mountain people. The sight of snow-capped peaks and alpine meadows does for their spirit what sunsets and sandy toes do for mine. My sister turned out to be one of those folks, and so did our son and his family. When I visit them, it takes me a day or two to catch my breath in that higher altitude. They tease me about always wearing a sweater, even in the middle of the summer.

On one of my trips to the mainland from Hawaii, I added an extra week so I could stay with our son and his family. The day before my travels, I was walking on the beach and found a perfectly intact whelk shell. It was about an inch long, ivory colored, with rows of smooth bumps. It came to a frosty cone swirl at the end. I put the little treasure in my pocket and decided to take it to our eldest grandson at his home in the mountains. He was only four years old at the time and already had a keen interest in nature and science. I thought he would like to see something that came fresh from the ocean.

When I presented him with the small gift, we had the sweetest conversation. He wanted to know all about the animal that once lived inside the shell and whether the emptied shell had come a long way before washing up on the shore. Together we made up a story and giggled over the names he gave to the sea-creature friends of the whelk.

That night, he slept with the shell under his pillow.

The next time I visited, he eagerly showed me where he kept the treasured shell in his bottom drawer. I had brought three more shells with me, along with a laminated chart I bought at a surf shop. The chart was designed for snorkelers to identify typical small sea creatures that lived in the coral reefs. With each image the name of the marine animal was printed; so together my clever grandson and I identified the species. We then had to make up more underwater adventure stories.

His shell collection grew over the next few years, every time I visited. More than once I told him how, whenever I walked on the beach, I always looked for special shells just for him. I also told him

that anytime I felt a little sad because I missed him so much, I would venture out to find another shell.

I loved having this shared joy with my grandson. I especially loved that the simple shells meant something special to both of us.

One time, while I was packing to leave after a short visit, he came into the guest room with all the shells in his hands. He lined them up on the bed and told me that whenever he looked at the shells, it helped him remember me and that made him feel happy. That made me very happy too.

The summer he was eight, I joined in on a family trip to the zoo during my stay. Even the zoo was built on a mountain slope, which apparently is an added delight for mountain people. My sea-level lungs were feeling it halfway through the day, so I opted to wait on a bench while the rest of the clan did a loop through the Great Apes building to see the orangutans again.

One cannot collect
all the beautiful shells on the beach.
One can collect only a few,
and they are more beautiful if they are few.
　　Anne Morrow Lindbergh

When they returned, my grandson had a shy grin on his face. "I missed you," he said. "So I looked until I found this."

He placed a small, smooth gray rock in the palm of my hand. A treasure from the mountain.

"Whenever you look at this rock, it will help you remember me and that will make you happy."

I wrapped my arms around him and held him tight. I wanted to tell him I would never need a rock or anything else to remember him. He was in my daily thoughts and prayers. But no words came out. Only a few tears.

He was right about one thing. His thoughtful gift has a place of prominence on my desk, and every time I look at that smooth pebble, it does make me happy.

But from everlasting to everlasting
the LORD's love is with those who
fear him, and his righteousness with
their children's children.

Psalm 103:17

I Started Early

I started early, took my dog,
And visited the sea;
The mermaids in the basement
Came out to look at me.

Emily Dickinson

get your vitamin sea

In case you need motivation to get yourself to the beach, may I share some reasons a day at the beach will be the best kindness you can show your weary self?

- Did you know that sunlight on our skin spikes our bodies' production of vitamin D? Sunshine also releases serotonin, which affects our nerve cells and elevates feelings of well-being and happiness. The message goes from our brains throughout our bodies.

- Listening to the ebb and flow of waves is a natural soother to our brains.

- Simply looking at the ocean activates receptors in the brain that release dopamine. Dopamine provides us with feelings of pleasure, satisfaction, and motivation. It helps us with memory, concentration, mood, and sleep.

- The color blue is known to trigger feelings of calm and peace.

- Focusing on the horizon, the thin line where blue meets blue, is known to hold our gaze and give our minds freedom to wander.

- Saltwater is detoxifying and rich in minerals that improve our skin as well as pull impurities from the body.

- Minerals found in ocean water include magnesium, zinc, iron, and potassium. These help to reduce inflammation and heal the skin as well as improve the flow of the lymphatic system.

Not convinced yet? Maybe this will motivate you: Research has shown that spending time on a beach eases depression and anxiety. Plus, sea air is proven to be a healing aid for lungs. Most importantly, your beach towel is tired of only spending time with your dog on bath days.

I could never stay long enough on the shore.
The tang of the untainted,
fresh and free sea air was like a cool,
quieting thought.

Helen Keller

The Love of God Is Greater Far

Could we with ink the ocean fill,
And were the skies of parchment made:
Were ev'ry stalk on earth a quill,
And ev'ryone a scribe by trade;
To write the love of God above
Would drain the ocean dry;
Nor could the scroll contain the whole,
Though stretched from sky to sky.

O love of God, how rich and pure!
How measureless and strong!
It shall forevermore endure
The saints' and angels' song.

Frederick M. Lehman

known

My grandmother owned a large queen conch shell. I have no idea where it came from. As a child, I thought it must be extremely rare. I would hold it to my ear so I could hear the ocean. For many years it resided on her small porch in rural Louisiana, next to a clay pot that sprouted red geraniums.

The queen conch has a new home on the deck of my California apartment, next to a pot of pink snapdragons. Sometimes my grandchildren pick it up and hold it to their ear. They nod when I ask if they can hear the ocean. I suspect they hear the same thing I heard. Just a slight swirl of air circling through the pink interior of the abandoned home of a sea snail that lived in it long ago, in some ocean far away.

One spring I was invited to go on a girls' getaway cruise to the Bahamas. I loved it! The luxurious cruise ship, the view of the Atlantic from our room's porthole, the thrill of docking at Nassau, and, of course, the fun time with the friends who accompanied me.

We noticed, as we strolled around Nassau, that conch was a popular food item at sidewalk cafés and food carts on the beach. If we wanted, we could order it raw in salads or cooked in "burgers," fritters, or gumbos. Images of my grandmother's conch shell came to mind, and like my friends, I passed on making a meal of a sea snail.

We planned to spend the afternoon in the clear turquoise water. We wanted to bob. To float and laugh and be drenched in sunshine. Other women from the cruise joined us, and the delight intensified as a gentle shower of warm tropical rain sprinkled down on us. The air, the water, and the rain all felt like they were the same temperature, and the sensation on our warm skin was luscious.

One by one, the other women paddled with wrinkled fingers back to the pristine white sand on the shore, ready for a leisurely nap beneath a welcoming cabana. I stayed in the water. So did one of my girlfriends. We floated near each other, but as was the custom of our sweet friendship, we didn't need to talk. As "high-functioning introverts," she and I valued the times we could simply share space. We didn't need to share words. We knew we had the freedom to close our eyes and get lost in our own thoughts and prayers while remaining only a few feet from each other.

The prayers that skimmed through my thoughts were about the talk I was scheduled to give that evening when we were back on the ship. Did my prepared notes cover what the women at this event needed to hear? Might the Lord want me to share something else?

I glanced at the island where the gorgeous white-and-blue-striped cabanas lined the shore. Then I turned back to the sea and shaded my eyes, taking in the image of the enormous cruise ship floating on the immense stretch of the Atlantic Ocean. Possibly my grandmother's queen conch shell had come from a place such as this. From this ocean. These waters. I thought of how far I was

It Is a Beauteous Evening

It is a beauteous evening, calm and free,
The holy time is quiet as a Nun
Breathless with adoration; the broad sun
Is sinking down in its tranquility;
The gentleness of heaven broods o'er the Sea.

William Wordsworth

from home and how much ocean lay beyond us on the edge of this tiny island.

As often happened when I fixed on such thoughts, I felt small. So tiny. Grain-of-sand small. Many times, I had squinted at an ocean and tried to imagine what lay beyond the horizon. When I did, a sense of the magnificence and enormity of God and His love for us caused me to feel miniscule.

That afternoon, however, a surprising and different sensation came over me.

Yes, God was immense and beyond comprehension, and yes, I was microscopic in His universe. But that day, in the same way the gentle raindrops had fallen on me, I felt covered by the truth that, in my tininess, I was known.

See what a lovely shell,
Small and pure as a pearl,
Lying close to my foot,
Frail, but a work divine,
Made so fairily well
With delicate spire and whorl,
How exquisitely minute,
A miracle of design!

      Alfred, Lord Tennyson

I was known, personally and intimately, by the Maker of the sea. The One who gathered the waters and set the tides in motion, the One who spoke the universe into being. He knew me. He called me by name.

The focus of my evening talk shifted. God was telling me something, and I wanted the women on the cruise to hear it as well. I returned to shore from my meditating, pulled my journal from my beach bag, and wrote as quickly as I could. I didn't want to lose any of the words I would pour out on the women that evening.

Before the molecules that formed you were gathered together, the Maker of the ocean depths knew you.

You.

He knows you.

Before your first breath, He began to lavish His love on you.

He put into motion all the purposes He desired to accomplish in you and through you during the days allotted to you on this earthly shore.

Before you even opened your eyes for the first time, He beckoned you to Himself. He placed you where He wanted you to be and with the people He wanted to raise you in this vast and mysterious and achingly beautiful world.

His magnificence rolls over the waves, over the water, just as it did in the beginning of all things when His Word tells us that His Spirit was brooding over the waters.

In the same way, His Spirit broods over you, dear fragile, eternal soul.

Right now.

He sees you. He knows you. He is creating something not yet known inside of you.

You are loved more than your splintered heart could ever imagine. He sees all your tears and catches every one of them in His bottle.

He wants you. He waits for you.

Come to Him. Draw near to God. He promises to draw near to you.

Tomorrow in the morning light, when you look out at the endless blue sea, may you sense the immenseness of His love for you. Instead of feeling like a small, insignificant human who has been set adrift on a wide, untamed ocean, may you remember that you are held in the everlasting arms.

You are wanted. You are known. He calls you by your name.

I shared those words on that delightful cruise years ago, but they came back to me today when I looked out the window at my grandmother's queen conch shell. More than ever, I treasure the truth that we are known by our gracious Heavenly Father. He still rains His unending love and grace on us every single day.

How Dear to Me the Hour

How dear to me the hour when daylight dies,
And sunbeams melt along the silent sea,
For then sweet dreams of other days arise,
And memory breathes her vesper sigh to thee.

And as I watch the line of light that plays
along the smooth wave toward the burning west,
I long to tread that golden path of rays,
and think 'twould lead to some bright isle of rest.

Thomas Moore

deep blue

mysteries of the vast ocean

So God created the great creatures of the sea
and every living thing with which the water teems and
that moves about in it... And God saw that it was good.
Genesis 1:21

under the sea

During my sophomore year of college, I signed up for a scuba diving class and was excited until I found out we would have to step off the high dive of the university pool in full scuba gear. I pressed through my fear of heights and completed the training. Our final exam for certification was held off the coast of the island of Catalina, and it became a life-changing day.

The adventure of boarding a boat in Long Beach and heading for the Catalina Marine Reserve was thrilling to my untraveled nineteen-year-old self. Experiencing the day with a close circle of classmates was exactly what great college memories are supposed to be about.

We set off on a beautiful spring day, and our friendly banter was as sparkling as the crystal tips of the waves in our wake. Once we were anchored and received our final instructions, I waited my turn to zip up my wet suit and take the plunge. It was a long way down to the water from the boat, but I knew I'd be fine if I didn't think about it. The other students went two by two, and none of them hesitated.

My name was called along with my buddy's name. We slipped our feet into our fins and checked our regulators. I was about to put my mask in place when our instructor stopped me. He pointed to a remarkable creature floating near the water's surface directly over the side of the boat. Our captain identified the marvel as a purple-striped jellyfish. It looked like a large white mushroom with evenly spaced purple lines radiating down the sides. As the invertebrate created leisurely fa-lopping motions, a long, delicate-looking appendage trailed from its center. The ivory tentacles reminded me of the tattered wedding veil of poor Miss Havisham in *Great Expectations*.

The beautiful jellyfish took its time. As we waited, I found my pulse had fallen into rhythm with its mesmerizing motions.

There is,
one knows not what
sweet mystery about this sea,
whose gently awful stirrings
seem to speak of some hidden soul beneath.

Herman Melville

Roll on, thou deep and dark blue Ocean—roll!

Lord Byron

My scuba buddy took the plunge off the side of the boat first. I watched and mentally went through the steps we had practiced for weeks.

When it was my turn, without a pinch of panic, I went over the edge, and our instructor followed. Aided by weight belts, we sank deeper and deeper into the hazy water until the sandy floor came into view below us. Our instructor pointed to the depth gauge on his wrist, indicating that we had hit forty feet and could begin the certification exam.

First, the instructor turned off the air supply from my buddy's tank. Could he restore the airflow? Yes. Success. My turn. Another success. Next, our masks were pulled from our faces, and we were to demonstrate how to put them back in place and clear out all the water. For a moment the saltwater pushed against my closed eyelids. A shiver of panic squeezed my lungs in the darkness.

Stay calm. Recall your training. Do what you were taught.

All valuable life lessons.

I felt around on the top of my head for my mask, straightened it over my eyes, and cleared the water. I blinked and saw the instructor give me a thumbs-up. The next steps in the exam were carried out one by one, and like all the other students in our class, my buddy and I passed.

In the happiness of our fresh success, we were now free to explore our foreign surroundings and had about fifteen minutes of air left before we needed to surface and return to the boat. We stayed side by side, legs extended, arms at our sides, fins propelling us. Our surroundings were nothing like the clear swimming pool where we had been taught. I wanted to stay in the underwater world as long as we could and take it all in.

Below us, in an open spot when the sunlight filtered through,

O LORD, what a variety of things you have made!
In wisdom you have made them all.
The earth is full of your creatures.
Here is the ocean, vast and wide,
teeming with life of every kind,
both large and small.

Psalm 104:24-25 NLT

I saw a shell sitting on a rock and thought it would make a grand souvenir. I indicated to my buddy that I was going deeper. My ears felt the pressure as I went down. The shell was within reach, but there was a problem. The inhabitant still occupied his vulnerable home! What was I thinking? Poor little guy. I'm sure he didn't appreciate me trying to pry him from his spot. I added one more instruction to myself: *Look but don't touch. I am the guest here under the sea.*

I turned around, looking for my buddy, and found that he had not followed me on my treasure hunt. Circling the area, I spotted his dark wet suit moving through a nearby forest of tall, wavy kelp. Most of him was concealed behind the thick growth, and I won-

dered if he was trying to be clever and hide from me.

With a few easy flips of my fins, I was close enough to reach out and tap his side. The grove of swaying stalks shook wildly the moment I touched him. It struck me that his wet suit didn't have the same texture as mine. Before I could consider why that was so, a cute gray face with black-button eyes and drooping whiskers popped through the seaweed and stared at me.

Our stunned responses were mutual. The California sea lion had not expected to see me, and I had not expected to see him!

Something touched my leg. I turned to see my buddy, pointing at the marvel in the forest of seaweed. I nodded and blinked away the tears of amazement before they could cloud my vision.

The sea lion pushed aside the curtain of kelp with his front flippers and came into plain view. We didn't move. He came a little closer and paused, examining us. Then, turning on his side, our new friend began to swim away. He paused, rotated to look at us again, and lingered a moment before moving on toward another area of thick, shifting kelp.

My winsome imagination believed he wanted us to follow him. To play hide-and-seek. To discover the wonders of his domain. My buddy didn't share my mermaid wishes and indicated by his hand signals that he was ready to surface.

Back on deck, his retelling of the encounter was factual. Scientific, almost. If I had been the first to speak, the account would have included much more description and all the elation I felt during our once-in-a-lifetime experience. I chose not to find another classmate to tell my version to. Instead, I kept my thoughts to myself.

On our ride back to the harbor, I sat alone, content to relive the experiences of the day. The sun slipped into the ocean the way an elegant woman steps into a waiting bath. The teal shades of the mysterious waters darkened, and the hues of the approaching land softened as a brisk breeze sent a misting of sea spray over the front of the boat. I felt as if I had entered Narnia and was sailing with Prince Caspian on the *Dawn Treader*.

As I watched the inky water below us, my view of God and His world continued to expand in my mind. I kept thinking about the verse that says, "No eye has seen, no ear has heard, and no mind has imagined what God has prepared for those who love him" (1 Corinthians 2:9 NLT).

Indeed, one feels microscopically small, and the thought that one may wrestle with this sea raises in one's imagination a thrill of apprehension, almost of fear.

Jack London

Even though the verse reads "No mind has imagined," I still tried to imagine the innumerable creatures hidden in the depths below us. I thought of all the subterranean ocean caverns where no human has ever been. What unseen wonders has God created, not only on this earth, but beyond our spinning blue planet? What secret phenomena are moving about at this moment in the universe?

When we arrived back at the harbor, I turned and took one long look at the ocean. A crescent moon had risen, slung in the sky like a

> The heart of man
> is very much like the sea,
> it has its storms, it has its tides
> and in its depths it has its pearls too.
>
> Vincent van Gogh

smile. A knowing smile, looking down on me in that sweet season of youth when I was choosing to trust God more and more.

Going under the sea that day led me to believe that I could trust Him for all the unseens and all the unknowns yet to be discovered. He was preparing things for me in the years ahead that I never could imagine.

here be dragons

"Here be dragons" appeared on a globe in the sixteenth century when no explanation could be given of what lies beyond the edge of the known ocean. Sailors and explorers were the astronauts of their time, venturing to faraway places and bringing back tales of what they had found.

One of those explorers stopped in the Canary Islands off the coast of West Africa for supplies before venturing across the Atlantic Ocean. A small, unassuming chapel in Las Palmas, on one of the primary islands, bears a plaque by the double wooden doors. In Spanish it reads "In this holy place Columbus prayed." I stood next to the sign and had my picture taken, as many tourists do, and tried to imagine what he prayed that night before setting sail into the unknown.

During my stay on the Canary Islands, my girlfriends and I were invited to visit the modest home of a flamenco dancer who lived by the beach. She went swimming in the ocean every day, and we were told to come after her morning dip. As we walked to her home, we paused to study a statue. As I took in the determined

The Secret of the Sea

My soul is full of longing
For the secret of the sea,
And the heart of the great ocean
Sends a thrilling pulse through me.

Henry Wadsworth Longfellow

expression on the woman's face, I imagined her to be the wife of a seaman because of the way she stood with hands on her hips, scanning the horizon, trying to catch a glimpse of her husband's ship returning to port. I wondered what the woman prayed while her love was away.

On arriving at the house, we noted that our seventy-two-year-old hostess had pushed back the furniture on her uneven tile floor. To our delight, she offered my friends and me a dance lesson.

"Stand up straight," our instructor said in Spanish. "One hand on your hip, the other in the air."

She demonstrated so that, even if we didn't know the Spanish terms, we would be able to imitate her.

"Chin up. Shoulders back." She struck a dramatic pose.

"Right foot, left foot. Again."

Stand up straight. One hand on your hip, the other in the air. Chin up. Shoulders back. Right foot, left foot. Again.

She watched as we repeated the steps and then shook her head. "No, no, no." Her finger was pointed at me.

"From the stomach up. You must feel it. Here. Like this. You must dance from the stomach up."

We tried again.

She singled me out and asked how old I was.

"Fifty," I told her.

She shook her head, clucked her tongue, and uttered a string of sentences that were beyond my ability to understand with my high school Spanish.

My friend translated. "She says that because you are only fifty, that is the problem. You are not old enough to dance flamenco. No woman can really dance flamenco until she is over sixty. This is because they have not lived enough, loved enough, or lost enough to dance from the stomach up."

The statue of the seafarer's wife came to mind. Like the uncharted sea, life and all its unknowns lie before all of us. Whether we are standing on the shore with hands on our hips, watching and waiting, or we are the ones braving the wild ocean, we are created to take risks and live fully that we might experience the exquisite emotions that come from fully living, loving, and losing.

Since that day, I have often thought of the words of our dance instructor. Especially around my birthday, when I'm about to add another year to the count. She convinced me that I did not want to spend any of my days trapped by a looming fear that "beyond here be dragons." Whenever I face an unknown or daunting challenge, I want to set sail through it with the intent of learning how to dance from the stomach up.

I also took to heart the message I read on the simple plaque by the door of the Las Palmas chapel. The best way to start a journey, whether on the shore or on the waves, is always with a prayer. Dragons, lurking in the unknown, whether real or imagined, can be slain.

He that will learn to pray, let him go to sea.

George Herbert

dutch masters

I don't know why my Dutch friends decided to take a detour on our way back to their home that Sunday afternoon. I was visiting them during a stretch of cold weather, and on such a cold and cloudy day, I would have welcomed a stop for a "cup of comfort." My friends had launched my new affection for dark Dutch coffee served in a small cup with a biscuit on the saucer. Why wouldn't that be our afternoon stop?

Instead, our destination was the North Sea. Just a quick "Hello, nice to meet you" visit, my friends explained to me.

On that day, parking wasn't a problem at the popular beach. I rolled up my pant legs, left my boots and socks in the car, which is also where my friends preferred to stay and wait for me. A wild gust met me when I opened the car door. I trotted and then sprinted down the walkway lined by tufts of seagrass.

Before me, the brown-sugar sands of Zandvoort Beach spilled out in a long stretch. I strode through the cold sand on the empty

My heart, and the sea, and the heaven
Are melting away with love!

Henry Wadsworth Longfellow

beach and headed for the shoreline. Every cell in me shivered. Every nerve went on high alert.

Yet the sea beckoned.

I planted my tingling feet on the wet shore and waited for the saltwater to wash over my feet. Shivers went through me, prompting me to laugh. Loudly. No one could hear me or see me as I danced in place. I kept laughing as the crisp wind tugged at my hair, bringing tears to my eyes and numbing my nose.

That was the moment I looked up and fully noticed the sky. It stretched over me like the landscape in the painting of a Dutch master. Distant and misty. All the base colors of aquamarine blues, ivory, and gray were applied with exquisite balance and blended flawlessly.

The visual feast, combined with the velocity of my emotions, filled me with a renewed hope and an unmistakable sense of my Master's presence.

My teeth were chattering from the cold. I needed to rush back to the car. But an elemental piece of me wanted to stay until I memorized the masterpiece of cloud patterns and the feathered layers of light radiating as the sun faintly pierced through the silken swath of sky. The pastel blues hinted at summer days to come, as did the sense of hope I'd felt in the middle of my twirl on the shore.

I ran most of the way to the car. Quickly shaking the sand off my bare feet, I opened the door and eagerly caught my breath as I settled into the warmth of the car. My face was rosy, my nose dripped, and I was shivering with elation. I didn't say more than a few words all the way to their home. My friends understood, I think. They let me sit quietly in the back seat, drenched in meeting the Master on the shore.

Your path led through the Red Sea.
You walked through the mighty waters.
But your footprints were not seen.

Psalm 77:19 NIRV

The Red Sea and Me

I have stood at the shore
of my own Red Sea
Felt the rumbling of chariots
Under my feet

I have left all behind
Crying out for more
I have followed and waited
Paralyzed on the shore

Between what once was
And what could yet be
My faith has faltered
At the edge of the sea

You, only You
Knew a way would appear
Where I saw no hope
You came so near

Fear not, You said.
Stand back and see
The Lord will fight for you
Just hold your peace

You did the impossible
You made a way
I stepped onto dry land
I did not delay

I did not doubt
Your care for me
I saw what You did
At my own Red Sea

Yet today I stand
On another rumbling shore
I want to believe
My foes will be no more

I try to remember
Your words, Do not fear
I know in my heart
You are so near

I'll wait and watch
believe and pray
I'll tell how You
delivered me again this day.

RJG

symphony of the sea

When we were living in the Pacific Northwest, our family of four, with two of those four being teenagers, needed to reconnect. Some friends offered us their family cottage by the sea, and off we went to the Oregon coast early on a Saturday morning in February.

My husband and I had stayed in the eighty-year-old cabin years earlier and were eager to relive some of the great memories of those summer days. We envisioned nights highlighted by stories around the firepit and hours of gazing up at the stars. Mornings would mean pancakes followed by scrambling down the hill to the tide pools. Afternoons would find us going into town for generous scoops of Tillamook Mudslide ice cream. We promised our teenage son and daughter all these perks after the long drive.

They weren't convinced that this was where they wanted to spend their weekend.

And neither were we when we arrived under a heavy canopy of gray clouds.

The cottage looked oh-so-much smaller than we had remembered.

Our descriptors of *quaint* and *remote* carried no charm for our children when they discovered we had no Wi-Fi.

"We're only here for one night," we repeated as we carried our bags into the musty dwelling. "Just wait until you see the view of the ocean from the front window."

My husband pulled up the bamboo blinds just as an army of pudgy raindrops threw themselves at the double-paned window. They seemed determined to block any view of the large patch of grass that ran to the cliff and the vast ocean beyond.

"A fire," I said. "That's what we need to cozy up this place."

The wood-burning stove in the corner cooperated nicely. I whispered a thank-you to the former guest who had left an unopened box of hot cocoa mix in the cupboard. Someone found a Monopoly game with all the pieces, and our family-bonding time commenced.

The storm continued to rise to an angst-driven crescendo followed by tense lulls of nothing but the wind instruments of nature. I said it was the "Symphony of the Sea," and we had box seats for the February performance. My attempt at giving our dismal adventure a touch of whimsy was not successful.

Dinner was meant to be cooked over the outdoor firepit along with s'mores. But the afternoon fog rolled in so thick we could barely see the firepit. Nightfall came quickly. The electricity flickered. We continued to feed the hungry stove and managed a few indoor s'mores, which also held little charm for our teens.

With all entertainment options explored and vetoed, we scavenged every blanket we could find, put on double socks, and bundled up in our vintage beds. For hours we listened to the unending symphony. The wind came from the north and bashed against

the cottage like a bully. The ocean foamed at the mouth and beat the rocky cliff with curled-up fists, punch after punch. I'd never seen this side of my old friend, the sea.

The long, thin fingers of the icy wind felt their way across the walls, searching for the tiny cracks around the rattling windows. They slid in, one by one, reaching for our ears, our noses, the napes of our necks. All night long the coastal storm carried on with its tantrum. Sleep came for each of us in uneven snatches. Morning light, dreary and flat, provided only enough motivation for me to get up, feed the fire, and light the small stove.

I found an old griddle that, once heated, smelled of every sourdough grilled-cheese sandwich and every slice of thick bacon that

Echoes

The sea laments
The livelong day,
Fringing its waste of sand;
Cries back the wind from the whispering shore—
No words I understand:
Yet echoes in my heart a voice,
As far, as near, as these—
The wind that weeps,
The solemn surge
Of strange and lonely seas.

Walter de la Mare

had ever touched its surface. The scent filled the tiny kitchen and wafted through the cottage, bringing an unexpected cheer from my hungry kin. Food was coming. Pancakes, to be specific. Pancakes with blueberries, Irish butter, and warm maple syrup.

The morning offering was uplifting enough to spark another round of Monopoly and an unsuccessful attempt at finding music on the old radio. A few smiles surfaced. Sweet teasing and old family jokes began. A brave sunbeam broke through the fog wall, pierced the front window, and shone like a spotlight on the tattered rug. Dozens of eager dust particles found partners and danced with abandon in the radiant stream of light.

At last, the lengthy score of this symphony was transitioning into the lively notes of the finale.

We watched as the outside world reappeared and dewdrop diamonds glistened on every quivery blade of grass. Soon, the subdued ocean revealed itself to us, like a field of emeralds stretching to the horizon. The last clouds scurried away on a breeze, and the sky came into view. Unobstructed indigo as far as we could see.

And he awoke and rebuked the wind
and said to the sea, "Peace! Be still!" And the
wind ceased, and there was a great calm.

Mark 4:39 ESV

"It's so pretty," our daughter said reverently.

We set out to explore the sunshine-kissed world of the new day and keep a few promises that included ice cream.

It's been years since our trip to the hideaway cottage. Each of us holds specific memories of the cold, the rattling of the wind at the door, the midnight pounding of the relentless sea, the pancakes, the tide pools, and who won both games of Monopoly. In the end, the time was good for us, that weekend we attended the "Symphony of the Sea." Never again have I heard such madly clashing cymbals, a more determined percussion section, or so many moody trombones dominating the brass.

Long scores of pounding sonatas may roll through our dark days and nights. But in the last movement, the soothing, airy flute notes of hope will arrive, carried on a sunbeam.

The sea, once it casts its spell, holds one in its net of wonder forever.

Jacques-Yves Cousteau

After the Rain

After the rain
serenity comes
tiptoeing through
the glistening trees

She flutters across
the humbled grass
shaking off the salty grudge
of the sated sea

Her breath
unhurried as a sleeping child
comes through my open door
with lulling fragrance sweet and wild

RJG

heavens to betsey

My love for Hawaiian history led me to discover a woman known by the name of Betsey Stockton. Born into slavery and living in Princeton, New Jersey, Betsey taught herself to read and was set free when she was eighteen. That same year, 1816, revival broke out on the Princeton University campus. Betsey attended a meeting, and her life was altered. She believed the love of God could be found only through salvation in Jesus Christ and that God's love was intended for the whole world.

She taught a Sunday school class for Black children and was allowed to take classes taught by a seminary student. He said she was more informed on biblical topics than anyone he had ever known.

Here's where Betsey's story stirred my heart.

She let it be known that she wanted to serve on a foreign mission field, but as a single woman, she was turned down for the position of being a teacher in Africa. However, another opportunity arose. One she gladly accepted.

On November 20, 1822, Betsey boarded a ship with thirteen other missionaries and sailed from New Haven, Connecticut, to the Hawaiian Islands. That would mean sailing all the way around South America, passing around Cape Horn, which separates Latin America from Antarctica. Can you imagine what such a journey would be like?

Fortunately, Betsey captured the experience in her journal, compiled during their 152-day voyage. Here are some of her remarkable descriptions of life at sea.

November 20, 1822, Departing New Haven, Connecticut

Here begins the history of things known only to those who have bid the American shores a long adieu.

November 22–23, Atlantic Ocean

In the night increased to a gale; seasickness increased with it. I was myself very sick. The water rushed into the cabin...I was so weak that I was almost unable to help myself. At 10 o'clock I went on deck: the scene that presented itself was, to me, the most sublime I ever witnessed. How, thought I, can "those who go down to the sea in ships" deny the existence of God?

December 25, Atlantic Ocean

Christmas. How unlike the last! But the day was pleasant, and...saw a large flock of flying fish. They rise from the water a little distance, when pursued by larger fish, and sometimes fly on board. They have a delicious flavor.

December 31, Atlantic Ocean

I was much interested in witnessing the harpooning of a large shark. It was taken at the stern of the ship, about 6 yards from the cabin window, from which I had a clear view. It was struck by two harpoons at the same time. The fish (if we may call it one, for it has very little the appearance of a fish) was so angry that he endeavored to bite the men after he was on deck. His jaw bone was taken out and preserved.

February 2, 1823, Atlantic Ocean

I am as happy as I ever was in my life.

If it were in my power, I would like to describe the phosphorescence of the sea. But to do this would require the pen of a Milton: and he, I think, would fail, were he to attempt it. I never saw any display of fireworks that equaled it for beauty. As far as we could see the ocean, in the wake of the ship, it appeared one sheet of fire, and exhibited figures of which you can form no idea.

February 5, Atlantic Ocean

All well and anxious to get round Cape Horn.

February 7, Off the Coast of Southern Argentina

Still sailing with all possible speed towards Cape Horn.

Just as the sun was setting, we were called to witness one of the most sublime scenes that ever the eyes of mortals beheld—no language could paint it—it was the setting of the sun. The scene kept changing from beautiful to more beautiful, until I could think of nothing but the bright worlds above, to which the saints are hastening.

As soon as it was over, and the sun had disappeared, we were assembled on the quarter deck for prayers. Here my soul found free access to the throne of grace and rose with delight in the contemplation of that God who is the author of all our joys, and of all good.

February 8, Tierra del Fuego

Our captain said nothing to us, but evidently appeared troubled. I then knew no danger and talked to him as usual—asked him to send a boat ashore; and jestingly told him, that I would accompany him. I thought he appeared very solemn and could give no reason for it.

The truth was that a strong current was drawing us towards these fatal rocks; and if wind enough should not rise to render the ship manageable, we must inevitably be wrecked upon them, during the ensuing night.

A fresh breeze sprung up towards evening, and we were soon borne beyond the reach of the current; but fresh dangers and anxieties awaited us.

February 9, Cape Horn

Here begins our tossing and rolling. Today we had rain and hail in squalls... The chance is ten to one that we are thrown across the cabin. I have had several pretty hard blows on my head... The wind was so strong that I could not stand without holding by my hands to something fixed: it seemed as if the ship was going on her beam ends every moment. This occurrence, however, did not intimidate me: I went on deck very often to view the grandeur of the sea; and it is truly one of the most sublime objects in creation. The sailors were always pleased to see me on deck in a storm and tried more than once to frighten me; but they found that they did not succeed.

March 1, Cape Horn

Twenty-one days ensued in which there was snow, hail, rain, and one continued gale. At times I have seen the waves rise mountains high before us; and it would appear as if we must inevitably be swallowed up; but in a moment our ship would rise upon the wave, and it would be seen receding at the stern.

I stayed on deck one evening until 12 o'clock, looking at the waves breaking over the ship: it was one of the most beautiful sights I ever beheld. The water would foam up like mountains of snow around us, and break over the deck; while below it sounded like thunder, or like rivers running over us.

I could compare our sailing when going before the wind to nothing but flying.

March 4, Pacific Ocean

We have completely doubled Cape Horn; the sea is much smoother.

March 26, Pacific Ocean

I felt as peaceful as the ocean with which I was surrounded. There not a wave was seen rising abruptly, from any part of our ship; all rolled smoothly

and gently along. *The succeeding night was beautiful beyond description; and all was peace within. I thought of St. John's "sea of glass mingled with fire," when I beheld the ocean... The full moon shone brightly on us, without one intervening cloud, while our vessel was wafted gently on the surface of the deep.*

It will be long before the impression of this evening will be erased from my mind.

March 30, Pacific Ocean

The first thing I heard in the morning, was that whales were seen spouting, off the stern. The captain ordered the course altered, and for two hours all was confusion and noise.

April 4, Pacific Ocean Approaching Hawaii

Nothing but pleasant weather followed, until we came in sight of Owhyhee [Hawaii]. We then had frequent squalls of rain, and hard blows; but not so as to make it uncomfortable.

Eternal Father, strong to save,
Whose arm does bind the restless wave,
Who bidd'st the mighty ocean deep
Its own appointed limits keep;
O hear us when we cry to Thee,
For those in peril on the sea!

       William Whiting

April 24, Honolulu, Hawaii

We saw and made Owhyhee...and as we sailed slowly past its windward side, we had a full view of all its grandeur. The tops of the mountains are hidden in the clouds.

May 28, Lahaina, Maui

Our place of worship was nothing but an open place on the beach, with a large tree to shelter us: on the ground a large mat was laid, on which the chief persons sat. To the right there was a sofa, and a number of chairs; on these the missionaries, the king, and principal persons sat. The kanakas, or lower class of people, sat on the ground in rows; leaving a passage open to the sea, from which the breeze was blowing...

After the service the favourite queen (Ka'ahumanu), called me, and requested that I should take a seat with her on the sofa, which I did, although I could say but a few words which she could understand.

The next morning, after the church service on the beach, Betsey made one of her final journal entries. She was approached by a boy who was a servant of the Hawaiian king, Liholiho. The boy said he wished to be instructed in English, and it was decided that Betsey should teach him. She rounded up six other Hawaiians and four English students. Classes began that day, and her school for commoners was established.

Betsey quickly became fluent in Hawaiian, and she trained her students to become teachers. Her time in Hawaii lasted until October 1825. She sailed to New England via London and became the most well-traveled Black woman at that time in history. In the two and a half years that she ran the school, she is credited with having taught eight thousand Hawaiians. When she returned to Princeton, she established a school for Black students and taught there for more than thirty years.

I like to think that along with teaching arithmetic, reading, and science, she also took time to tell her students tales of the sea and of the faraway Hawaiian Islands.

They were glad when it grew calm,
and he guided them to their desired haven.
Let them give thanks to the LORD for his
unfailing love and his wonderful deeds
for mankind.

Psalm 107:30–31

The Golden Hour

*How calm, how beautiful comes on
The stilly hour, when storms are gone;
When warring winds have died away,
And clouds, beneath the glancing ray,
Melt off, and leave the land and sea
Sleeping in bright tranquility—*

*Fresh as if Day again were born
Again upon the lap of Morn!
When the light blossoms, rudely torn
And scatter'd at the whirlwind's will,
Hang floating in the pure air still,
Filling it all with precious balm,*

*In gratitude for this sweet calm—
And every drop the thunder-showers
Have left upon the grass and flowers
Sparkles, as 'twere that lightning-gem
Whose liquid flame is born of them!*

Thomas Moore

peace be still

I should have known. I should have remembered God's faithfulness. I should have trusted. But I didn't. My heart filled with fear before we even arrived in Brazil.

Four days before our scheduled flight, I had a root canal, and within hours my face swelled, and the pain was unbearable. Three days before our departure, I knew something clearly was wrong. The endodontist prescribed an antibiotic, to which I had an allergic reaction that put me in the hospital on a heart monitor.

Two days before we were supposed to leave, I was home in bed, on a different round of medications and sedated. We would have to cancel the trip. I couldn't board a plane like this. And I certainly couldn't speak at the many venues the Brazilian publisher had set up on the book tour to four different cities. Not when my mouth was still too sore to eat, and my face looked like a puffer fish.

The morning of our flight, as planned, I went to the endodontist at 7:00 a.m. He examined my molar, checked my vitals, asked how I was doing on the new meds, and decided I was stable enough to go on the three-week trip. His wife was from Brazil. "You'll love it," he said. "Be sure to go to the beach."

I was so certain that he would advise against travel that I had done nothing to prepare for our 11:30 a.m. flight. Hurrying home, my husband and I packed in a flurry and made it to the airport on time. I don't remember anything about the nineteen-hour flight. I do remember being picked up by our enthusiastic host and how he insisted on driving in crazy traffic to take us to see the Christ the Redeemer statue before we did anything else.

In the mad scurry, a car swerved and crashed into us, caving in the front door where my husband was sitting. We were okay but didn't understand why our host stopped in the middle of the busy highway and got out of the car. The driver who hit us did the same. We watched as the two men checked the damage while a stream of angry drivers honked and passed us.

Then he asked them, "Where is your faith?"
The disciples were terrified and amazed.
"Who is this man?" they asked each other.
"When he gives a command, even the wind and waves obey him!"

Luke 8:25 NLT

Our driver returned, started the engine, and drove on. Insurance cards hadn't been exchanged. A police report wasn't made. Why? Our host shrugged, saying that the damage to both cars was about the same, so they had shaken hands and walked away, saying, "Let's not let this ruin our day."

We remained speechless and attentive on the narrow, winding road to the top of Mount Corcovado. Our host stayed with the car to protect our luggage while we took a recently installed escalator up to where the statue stood so we could experience a close-up view. Spider monkeys hung from the trees lining our ascent, and once again, I was reminded that we weren't in the United States anymore.

When we stood in the great shadow of the famous Christ the Redeemer architectural wonder, I struggled to take in the monument. The nearly one-hundred-year-old, ninety-eight-foot-high concrete sculpture had been added to the modern list of the Seven Wonders of the World in 2007, and I saw why. The magnificent structure was covered with more than six million triangular tiles made of soapstone. I had read that some of the tiles contained notes and prayers written on the reverse side by the workers before affixing them. As a work of art, it was astounding. Its position on the mountaintop was breathtaking. From where we stood, we tried to take in the spectacular view of the coastline and beaches of Rio de Janeiro.

Our visit was brief, and as soon as we were back in the car, our host said we had a choice. He could drive us down to the beach or take us to the hotel where we could order some food. If we chose to take a short walk along Copacabana Beach, we would have to go straight to the bookstore for the first book signing. We would eat later. And, he mentioned, this would be our only chance to see the famous beaches of Ipanema and Copacabana.

Lines Composed in a Wood on a Windy Day

My soul is awakened, my spirit is soaring
And carried aloft on the wings of the breeze;
For above and around me the wild wind is roaring,
Arousing to rapture the earth and the seas...

I wish I could see how the ocean is lashing
The foam of its billows to whirlwinds of spray;
I wish I could see how its proud waves are dashing,
And hear the wild roar of their thunder to-day!

Anne Brontë

I thought of what the endodontist said. My husband indicated he wanted to walk on the beach. I always want to go to the beach, so the choice was made.

We slipped out of our shoes and socks and carried them past the rows of sand volleyball courts where stellar athletes were enjoying their rigorous games. With quick strides through the sand, we wove our way across the crowded beach and finally stopped in an open area where we could look out at the water. The wind was up, and the waves were choppy. The air carried with it recognizable tinges of a storm coming.

I thought the familiar feeling of sand between my toes and the taste of salt clinging to my lips would bring a much-needed sense of calm to my racing heart. But I still felt anxious, lost, and at the mercy of everything going on around me.

Then, as if my battered thoughts weren't shuffled enough, the overload of new sensations broke through the false wall of courage I had erected when the endodontist said, "You'll be fine." I gave way to fear and reached for my husband's hand, squeezing it hard. Why were we here? What did it matter? Could God's plan really include an exploded root canal, a car accident, monkeys, and an approaching storm?

I turned my face back toward the land, trying to keep the whipped-up sand from blowing into my eyes.

There in the distance, with arms outstretched, was the statue of Jesus. He had looked so different when I was at His feet. So accessible. So endearing, covered in prayers hidden behind the tiles. He appeared mighty and loomed with a presence that couldn't be ignored when we were up close. Now the statue, and also the presence of His Spirit, seemed far away.

> There is one spectacle
>   grander than the sea,
> that is the sky;
>   there is one spectacle
> grander than the sky,
>   that is the interior of the soul.
>
> Victor Hugo

Like a clueless disciple bailing water, I was rocking about in my own small boat of circumstances. Just as the disciples asked Jesus if He even cared about them, I wondered the same. They thought the storm at sea was about to capsize them. I understood their fear because, in that moment, I was at the mercy of external conditions raging around me. I felt like the waves of my emotions were about to capsize me.

Jesus spoke to the storm when He was with the disciples.

On the beach in Brazil, He spoke to the storm raging inside me. *Peace. Be still.*

I looked up once again at the statue of Christ the Redeemer before we walked back to the car still holding hands. I thought of how Jesus's friends asked themselves, "Who is He, that even the wind and

the waves obey Him?" I wondered if I, too, had any idea how great the power of my Redeemer was. My jitters settled, and my heart slowed its frantic pace. I can't explain why or how, but the fear had to leave when I focused on Jesus.

He was with us the entire trip. We saw Him do amazing things. My tooth never bothered me. And my endodontist was right. I loved Brazil. I loved the people.

That trip had a widespread and amazing impact on many of the teen girls I met on our tour. Years later, when it was easy to translate online, letters poured in from those girls telling me how they came to know Christ after reading one of my books translated into Portuguese by the Brazilian publisher. A number of them said they decided to become writers after hearing me speak. They sent me copies of their published, Christ-honoring novels. I met a few of them in California, when they came to the States for a visit with their young families. The repeated message from all those beautiful, eternal souls is that their adventure with Jesus began as a result of my trip to Brazil.

Why did I ever doubt?

He is with us. He still commands the winds and waves of our lives.

Peace. Be still.

But LORD, you are more powerful than the roar of the ocean. You are stronger than the waves of the sea.

Psalm 93:4 NIRV

Sea Sonnet

Above the ocean the clouds
form a single line
like preschoolers grasping a long rope
merrily off on a field trip.

The whitecaps across the waters
catch the sunrise
sparkling with a thousand whispers
captured in time like diamonds.

I watch as You write Your love sonnet
with every stroke of the tides
holding creation in the palm of Your hand,
dictating Your faithfulness on the wind.

RJG

island
dreams

tropical bliss

GOD's my island hideaway,
keeps danger far from the shore,
throws garlands of hosannas around my neck.
Psalm 32:7 MSG

hololani

The year my husband and I married, his parents bought a beach-front condo on Maui. The two-bedroom unit was on the sixth floor of a complex called Hololani, which means "gone to heaven." The family condo fulfilled its name for many years. We always felt as if we were experiencing a taste of heaven when we entered this haven for weary minds and bodies.

The lanai, or front deck, of the condo was wide enough for a round table that fit six if we sat close. A chaise lounge served as the best place to lie back and gaze at the beautiful blue ocean, which stretched out in front of the viewer. The island of Molokai was only nine miles away and loomed large and sometimes foreboding when rain clouds gathered around its highest peaks. To the left was the island of Lanai. During the winter months, the whales always returned. Both the mother whales and the newborn calves would joyfully breech and do tail slaps in their beautiful blue playground while catamarans, windsurfers, and outrigger canoes skimmed across the expanse.

A Touch of Paradise

A touch of paradise is all I ask
to keep my spirits high
A trade wind breeze about my knees
a gray dove's gentle cry

The push of a swim, the burning sun,
fish beneath the sea
Love was there and friends were there
to keep me company.

Sun-flecked blue, fishnet globe
buoyant in the ocean's foaming swell
awesome breakers consuming coral reefs
a story long to tell

Sunlit blue, starlit nights
with tropic song that dances to its grace
the strings of life come pulsing back
to show my Father's face

And when it's gone my heart will ache
for islands' perfumed air
O, may I walk with you again
wild jasmine in your hair?

Robert Greenwald

Every time we returned, the first thing we did was open the sliding door and step out on the lanai. I often whispered a prayer of gratefulness as we welcomed the rustling of the trade winds in the palm trees and listened to the waves as they trimmed the caramel-colored sand with a thin, wavy line of froth. Sleeping with the doors open meant falling asleep to the melody of the waves every single night.

Bliss.

One Christmas, before my husband and I had children, the Gunn clan gathered at the condo. My mother-in-law determined we needed a Christmas tree. Our trips into town were without success. The Matson container that had arrived by cargo ship a week earlier had rapidly emptied of the Oregon-grown evergreens.

Undaunted, she made a jaunt to the local farmers' market seeking inside info from locals. She returned with fresh papaya and a three-foot, triangular macramé wall hanging. The woman at the craft table assured her that the wall hanging was the best she'd be able to come up with since Christmas was only two days away.

A nail was sledged into the wall, and our tropical substitute for a Tannenbaum was hung with lots of smiles and some teasing.

The next year we arrived a week before Christmas, and that meant we were in time to purchase one of the last real Christmas trees from the lot near the airport. My mother-in-law was happy with our victorious find until we discovered the tree was too big to fit inside the condo.

Undaunted, we hauled it through the living room and set it up on the lanai where I spun an excess of colorful lights around it.

Our tradition was to take family walks down the beach at sunset. That Christmas we made sure to plug in the lights so that we could fully admire our large twinkling tree on the lanai as we walked back to the condo. I wouldn't be surprised if night fishermen off the coast of Molokai could see our tree.

Within four days, all the dried out, wind-tossed pine needles had fallen off, making a grand mess and leaving an assortment of flopping branches heavily ladened with lights. More joking ensued, and the macramé tree was hung on the wall to save us from the large Charlie Brown Christmas tree on the lanai.

More Christmases on Maui followed, as well as vacations and getaways any chance we could get. I became a master at collecting air mileage points.

Our son was two years old when he took his first flight across the sea to our island hideaway. He became a natural in the water and still is the first one in and the last one out of the waves.

Our daughter was only six months old when she felt the warm Maui water tickle her toes. She, too, seemed right at home, and still is.

When an opportunity arose for my husband to take a sabbatical, we knew where we wanted to spend those nine months. We happily put our belongings in storage and volunteered to do a long list of renovations needed at the aging condo. Projects such as scraping popcorn ceilings, painting, replacing flooring, and installing bathroom tile were fixtures on the list.

We enrolled our son in third grade at Kamehameha Elementary School in Lahaina for the school year. Every Friday my blond boy and I rose earlier than on other weekday mornings when he caught the school bus. Instead, on Fridays, I drove him into Lahaina, where we would be the first customers of the day at the old Pioneer Inn, a restaurant by the harbor. Breakfast was always macadamia nut pancakes with coconut syrup. Conversations were always

Home of My Heart

No other sky
than this canopy of azure blue
No other green
than this cascade of crushed emeralds
No other gold
than Makena sand between my toes
No other song
than trade winds in the coconut palms
No other home
than this island anchored in the deep blue sea.

RJG

sweet and silly. A few times he held my hand as we took the short-cut to school by walking underneath the banyan tree. He would let go long before we reached the playground, but my heart never let go of those Friday mornings.

My parents came to visit during our sabbatical stretch at Hololani. One morning I took a picture of the beach while standing on the lanai. I used a disposable camera, and the results weren't great, but I love that picture. To the left, under the shade of a leaning palm tree, a tall figure is bending over something in the sand. Two small figures are close by, busily at work. No one understood why I framed the fuzzy photo and kept it on my

Trade Winds

Now come the trades
on ancient paths unseen
with silken ribbons of heart-spun dreams
softly brushing against my skin
whispering of what might have been.
I close my eyes
and dream again.

RJG

bookshelf for years. We had a dozen other photos of the beach and ocean taken from the same spot that were much better. But, you see, this was the only image of my dad and my children building castles together in the sand.

We returned one Christmas when our kids were teenagers. We had made it clear that the trip and the chance to simply be at Hololani were their gifts that year. No presents would be stacked up under a tree. They were fine with that until our second day there when our daughter said it just didn't feel like Christmas. She asked if we could at least buy a tree. A small one.

"Come with me," I said. We ventured to the underground parking garage and opened the storage box in our assigned stall. Behind the tubs of spackle and a spare shower curtain, I found what I was hoping was still there—the macramé tree safely wrapped in a garbage bag. In my mother-in-law's handwriting, it was labeled with the Hawaiian words for "Merry Christmas," *Mele Kalikimaka.*

Our thirteen-year-old daughter didn't remember the tree. Nor did she remember much about her grandma. But the artist in her teenage soul loved the crafty tree. She was thrilled to hang it on the nail that still protruded from the wall. The tree was soon adorned with ornaments she made from flowers, shells, and leaves. Every morning when I stepped into the living room and saw it on the wall, I smiled.

Over the decades, our visits to the condo often included friends from the mainland. Many returned to Hololani for their own family vacations, saying they couldn't stop dreaming of the views and the warm, plumeria-scented air. We felt the same way. That's why, when my father-in-law chose to sell the condo, we weren't the only ones to shed a tear over the loss. I was certain our dreamy days and star-filled nights on Maui would be snuffed out for good.

Then a God thing happened. It's the only way to explain it. Our son was married and our daughter engaged when an unexpected opportunity came for my husband and me to move to Maui. We weren't ready to retire, but we both had mobile careers. So we sold our home of the past sixteen years and settled on the south shore of our beloved island.

We were thrilled when our daughter and her new husband moved down the street a few years later. Their first son was born on Maui. He was only a few months old when I watched his toes wiggle in the sand for the first time.

That Christmas, our next-generation family of five strung twinkle lights on the palm tree in the front yard of our little yellow house and went swimming in the ocean on Christmas morning. Brunch and gifts were at our daughter's apartment. I entered with a tray of fresh papaya, pineapple, and batter for macadamia nut pancakes.

The sliding door of their second-floor condo was open all the way. The salty sea air swirled through the small room and stirred the sweet fragrance arising from a bouquet of tuberose. On the wall, in a place of prominence, hung the faded green macramé Christmas tree, decorated with handmade ornaments, old and new.

For a moment, I thought I'd gone to heaven. 🌴

A Day of Sunshine

O gift of God! O perfect day:
Whereon shall no man work, but play;
Whereon it is enough for me,
Not to be doing, but to be...

And over me unrolls on high
The splendid scenery of the sky,
Where through a sapphire sea the sun
Sails like a golden galleon,

Towards yonder cloud-land in the West,
Towards yonder Islands of the Blest.

Henry Wadsworth Longfellow

fifty-two saturdays by the sea

Before our daughter and her husband moved to Maui, we lived thousands of miles apart. I keenly felt that separation for the seven years she was in college and then working and rooming with friends before marrying. After she and her husband settled into their new island life, she and I launched a yearly goal of spending fifty-two Saturday mornings together at the beach.

I would watch my phone on Saturday mornings, waiting for her text saying, *On my way*, and I would feel giddy.

After I wiggled into my bathing suit, she would swing by to pick me up. No makeup, hair a fright, we stopped for coffee and croissants in Wailea and then drove a few more miles to "our" beach. One of us was always midstory, sharing details of our week, as we navigated the short hike through the kiawe woods. We laughed. We listened.

In May, our passageway was alive with flitting yellow butterflies. As we drew closer to the shore, we were greeted by the familiar call of the waves. With grateful surrender, we nestled into

I will awaken the dawn.
I will praise you, LORD, among the nations;
I will sing of you among the peoples.
For great is your love, higher than the heavens;
your faithfulness reaches to the skies.

Psalm 108:2-4

the brown-sugar sand where we sipped our lattes and broke bread together. We were the only ones on the beach.

The sun rose over the massive top of the Haleakala volcanic crater and turned the red earth of the neighboring island of Kahoolawe into a burnished gem set adrift in an azure sea.

Always, in that moment, we were God's biggest fans. He took our breath away.

Stories were paused. The foibles of the previous week were forgotten. We began to breathe again, deeply. Unrushed. Undone.

We gawked.

We were home.

This golden beach was our spot on this wild, spinning planet. We knew the winds, the clouds, and the rains of this place.

We recognized the funny head of the granddaddy sea turtle who favored these morning waters in the springtime. We knew the local boys who lined up on their boards in the white curling spray of the big waves of summer.

We knew the winter calm, when the waters appear translucent, and we floated with our painted toenails bobbing in front of us like too many cherries in a salty Shirley Temple.

We knew that, when autumn came, the south swell would roll in with a gang of brazen waves that love to make fists and pound the shore, leaving broken bits of shells in long wavy lines.

Sea crumbs, my daughter called them.

When the bully waves of October came, we scavenged sea crumbs as if they were memories we had dropped or promises we had forgotten. We knew the persistent housekeeper, the tide, would sweep them out to sea at sunset. But we arrived long before her shift began, and the sea crumbs were ours for the taking.

Side by side we walked, trolling the shore. Our sandy palms filled with simple offerings of the lovely shards that we showed to each other, heads bent in earnest. We held pieces of polished white coral. Unbroken puka shells. Smooth blue and green sea glass, one of them the size of an engagement diamond.

These castoffs of the mermaids became our tiny treasures. They filled small bottles and miniature glass jars that lined our kitchen windowsills. They glowed in the afternoon sunlight.

Visitors arrived and spread their towels on the cashmere sands. Sunbeams rested on our shoulders with convincing warmth. We would saunter back to the car with our fresh catch of oodles of sea crumbs. They jingled in my emptied coffee cup, sounding like coins. Many coins, rubbing together.

I felt rich.

Rich in moments of secrets shared, expressions captured, tears shed, giggles, and guffaws. During our year's saunter through fifty-two Saturdays by the sea, I was given the gift of meeting the adult version of my only daughter and being welcomed as her friend.

Perhaps this is the most important
thing for me to take back from beach-living:
simply the memory that
each cycle of the tide is valid;...
each cycle of a
relationship is valid.

Anne Morrow Lindbergh

Your Love

*Your love is constant
like the waves
gentle, unhurried
rolling over the shore
seamless
ancient and
new
every morning.*

RJG

dolphins

We knew when my husband and I went to New Zealand that it had become a destination for fans of the Narnia and Lord of the Rings films. On the North Island, visitors can tour the movie set of Hobbiton and explore the ruins of Cair Paravel. On the South Island, the setting for the capital city of Rohan awaits eager devotees.

However, we didn't make a trek to the Elephant Rocks of Aslan's Camp, nor did we include a tour day at Matamata for the thrill of ducking through one of the rounded hobbit doors and picturing Bilbo Baggins sitting by the fire.

Instead, we had another small adventure.

On the advice of a friend who favored the South Island, we took the Coastal Pacific train from Christchurch to Picton and rode the scenic ferry across Cook Strait to Wellington on the North Island. The views of the ocean and the landscape on that clear, sunny day were beyond any movie set involving fauns or hobbits.

The train left Christchurch at 7:00 a.m. sharp. Every time

we rounded a bend it seemed we were invited to take in another precisely angled, unobstructed view of the ocean. The Pacific presented herself that day draped in shimmering royal-blue sapphires. She looked stunning and otherworldly.

The farther we went up the coast, the more our attention swiveled from the ocean view to the land view. The snowcapped Inland Kaikoura Mountains appeared daunting and breathtaking. Their ninety-seven jagged and varied peaks presented ever-changing views as the clouds floated by. The mountains continued to run parallel to the sea for nearly an hour of our trip.

I guess, as a writer, I felt compelled to capture the moment by recording something in my travel journal. Strangely, I could find no words to describe the beauty. The views were like nothing I'd ever seen before. I didn't want to look down at my pen and paper.

The castle of Cair Paravel on its little hill towered up above them; before them were the sands, with rocks and little pools of salt water, and seaweed, and the smell of the sea and long miles of bluish-green waves breaking for ever and ever on the beach. And oh, the cry of the seagulls! Have you heard it? Can you remember?

C.S. Lewis

The landscape on both sides of the train required my full and adoring attention.

About halfway through the five-and-a-half-hour journey, the train stopped somewhere along the shore in the Canterbury region. We were invited to disembark for a quick stretch. Our stop was close to a large bay where we could see that the surf was up. My husband and I told the conductor we were going to make a dash down to the water. He told us to be quick about it.

We made our way down a worn path on a grassy slope and wove through the driftwood and smooth stones on the beach. At the water's edge we stood together, breathing in the fresh sea air. The sun came at us like a searchlight. Even with sunglasses, we had to shield our eyes. It was worth it to try to get a fix on the waves because the sunlight turned the rising wave into a translucent, aquamarine wall of seawater.

As the waves rose, we spotted dolphins. Three. Then five. Then eight. They were lined up, inside the curl of the wave, with their long noses pointed toward us on the shore. Taking one bold wave after another, the dolphins continued to frolic, and we continued to smile and stare, speechless.

If this had been a tour of a movie set and the dolphins had been an added CG effect, it would almost have been easier to comprehend what we were seeing. But this was real life. Those were real dolphins. The angle of the light and the lavish colors were chosen by God, not by the director of photography.

We didn't even think to take a picture. The same way that I couldn't find words to describe the scenery in my journal, I don't think either of us could find a way to fully absorb the sight of the dolphins playing in the Pacific Ocean that day as we watched them from that pebbled shore.

The train whistle sounded, and we rushed to continue our journey. We settled in our seats, hearts pounding and breathless. All I could think of was what God said so simply in the first chapter of His book: "And God saw that it was good" (Genesis 1:25).

He stirs up the ocean.
He makes its waves roar.
His name is the LORD Who Rules Over All.

Jeremiah 31:35 NIRV

Address to the Ocean

O, wonderful thou art, great element...
And lovely in repose! thy summer form
Is beautiful, and when thy silver waves
Make music in earth's dark and winding caves,
I love to wander on thy pebbled beach,
Marking the sunlight at the evening hour,
And hearken to the thoughts thy waters teach,—
Eternity—Eternity—and Power.

Bryan Waller Procter

island sand

I couldn't take my eyes off the large picture at the art exhibit. "It's sand," the photographer-artist told me. "Sand that has been magnified five hundred times and shot through a special microscopic lens."

The bright colors and distinct shapes astounded me. All those bits of incredible variation were under my bare feet every time I strolled along the shore. His work was breathtaking, and so was the price. Otherwise, one of those beauties would have come home with me and found a wall where I could look at it over and over.

That visual feast of the minute granules prompted me to learn more about sand. I discovered some fascinating details.

Did you know that sand is made of decomposed rocks and tiny crystals of mineral quartz from different kinds of sedimentary and igneous rocks, as well as from bits of shells, coral, glass, and marine organisms?

The most surprising ingredient in sand is fish excrement. I heard that fun fact from a sea captain on a Maui snorkeling trip,

> How precious are your thoughts about me, O God.
> They cannot be numbered!
> I can't even count them;
> they outnumber the grains of sand!
>
> Psalm 139:17-18 NLT

but I thought he was kidding. Parrotfish eat coral, grind it up, and expel it. It's estimated that 70 percent of the sand on white beaches comes from this natural process. So, when you walk on a white sandy beach, you'll know that the white comes mostly from coral— and now you know where the coral came from.

Sorry.

Did you also know that islands around the world have beaches with different colors of sand?

Black sand comes from lava. When the lava flows into the ocean, it immediately cools and is eroded into tiny granules that are washed ashore. Sea turtles prefer black sand beaches because the black sand is warmer than white sand. (And maybe turtles know where the white sand came from.)

Red sand is formed when the lava cools before it hits the ocean. The high iron content in the lava oxidizes and turns the rocks red before they are worn down into small sand particles.

Only four green sand beaches exist in the world. One of them is at the southern tip of the Big Island of Hawaii. Certain kinds of volcanic eruptions can bring crystals to the surface, and green sand is created. This happens when the lava shatters as it touches the cool ocean water and tiny crystals are formed.

No one knows an exact number, of course, but millions upon millions of grains of sand are in every cubic meter of beach.

Here's the most fun fact of all.

No two grains of sand are alike.

I've never seen a red sand beach, and although I've been on the Big Island of Hawaii, I didn't attempt to visit the green sand beach. It's remote and difficult to access, which makes it even more of a one-of-a-kind beach.

We have explored the black sand beach on Maui a number of times. Several times we stayed overnight at the cabins in the state park the beach is a part of. One of those times we were with another family. Between us we had five teenagers. The kids took the bunks, and the parents opted to sleep on the floor in the kitchen area on air mattresses. Our two queen-sized mattresses filled the space. No blankets were needed on that tropical night.

Lights were out. Kids had stopped talking. We all fell fast asleep after the long drive on the Hana Highway.

In the morning, we shook the papaya tree next to the cabin and caught our breakfast. The kids trekked down to the black sand and waded into the blue water. When we arrived, the view was otherworldly. Black sand, blue ocean, green tropical foliage, white clouds dotting the sky.

In the same way that no two grains of sand are alike, the contrast of being on a black sand beach made me realize that no two beaches are alike. No two days are alike. And no two experiences are the same. I think that is what compels us to go, see, do, and experience all kinds of new adventures. In every moment we are invited to see up close the artistry and magnificence of God's designs.

I could look at sand of all colors under a microscope all day.

The day awakening, drowsily opening its
eyes ... The sea froths into patterns of foamy
lace and slides back with a soft sighing ...
hold the moment ...
the day is yours to take as you will.

Don Blanding

beach wedding

Lunch with a friend at one of the beachfront restaurants on Maui was always a treat. One particular café became our go-to whenever one of our circle of friends was having a birthday. We even had a preferred outdoor table that was only steps from the sand and the sea.

At one such birthday gathering, we were seated at our favorite spot and intrigued to see that everything had been set up for a beach wedding only a few yards away. The white folding chairs were neatly lined up. Pretty island ferns and bright purple orchids were tucked into an archway that looked like an enchanting door opening to the sea.

We hadn't even placed our orders when the guests arrived and filled the chairs. A local minister some of us recognized took his place under the arch. The groom looked handsome in his black tux worn island-style with the tie missing and the first few shirt buttons open.

On the Fifth Day

God filled the salty waters
With great whales and fish galore
Then he told the foaming waves
To run and kiss the shore

RJG

The musician for the ceremony stood to the side and played a familiar song on a ukulele as the guests awaited the bride's arrival. She approached the gathering, wearing a simple white gown with a *lei po'o*, a wreath of white flowers, on her head and a small bouquet of island greenery, white gardenias, and orchids in her hand.

We tried not to stare, but we observed the groom's teary-eyed smile as his wife-to-be stood in place, smiling at him and waiting for the music to change to her processional song. As the first notes began, her mother stood in the front row, and all the guests rose and turned toward the beautiful bride.

She was about to take her first step down the flower-strewn sandy path when a woman at the table next to ours suddenly pointed to the ocean and loudly exclaimed, "Oh my!"

I turned to see a whale breeching close enough to shore for everyone to observe her wide berth as the big mama came down with a thunderous splash. The wedding guests turned to look. Diners stood and pulled out their phones. Even the groom and minister turned their backs to the bride. The music stopped, and all eyes were now on the water as the whale breeched again and then again. You could hear the momentous slap of her enormous broadside as it hit the water.

The most adorable sight followed. The whale's small protégé surfaced and did a little hop out of the ocean and right back in. The baby whale did it again, this time catching more air, and then a third time. The mother whale demonstrated the full technique again, and four times in a row the baby whale leapt into the air and did an impressive splashdown. It was the cutest, most amazing sight.

Akamai Island Breeze

I hear you,
gentle morning breeze
threading through the mango trees.

A hint of pikake
lingers on your breath, evidence
of where your night was spent.

Come, I beg,
Keep company with me.

You pause, as coy as coy can be,
then gather your skirts
and rush to the sea.

The waves rise up, eager to receive
your morning kisses,
You flirty island breeze.

RJG

There before me lies the mighty ocean, teeming with life of every kind, both great and small… And over there, the whale you made to play in the sea. Every one of these depends on you to give them daily food.

Psalm 104:25-27 TLB

I glanced at the bride. She stood at the end of the aisle waiting, shoulders stooped, bouquet down to her side. My heart went out to her. This was her day and her moment. She had been upstaged by a baby whale.

Every wedding guest, the minister, the groom, and diners at all the tables watched—and several waiters had even stopped in place, holding dishes they had just cleared. Sweet sounds rose from all the spectators the way a chummy crowd cheers for a spectacular fireworks display, including well-placed oohs and aahs.

The mama and baby practiced two more leaps and splashes, and then they submerged.

For a moment it seemed as if everyone within sight was shaking themselves to return to where they were before the captivating spectacle took our breath away.

The musician strummed the processional song again. The groom and minister turned around, and the guests shifted back to bride-viewing position, some turning their phones to film her now that the sea show had ended.

The bride didn't move. She lifted her chin, straightened her shoulders, and then she burst out laughing. The sweet laugh caused a contagious ripple effect through not only the surprised wedding guests but also the restaurant guests. Ours was a discreet echo of the merriment that encompassed the wedding.

Such joy.

What a lovely way to walk down the aisle and into your future with the love of your life. Surrounded by laughter, family, friends, and the shared experience of an everyday miracle of new life.

To Jane: The Recollections

The whispering waves were half asleep,
The clouds were gone to play,
And on the bosom of the deep
The smile of Heaven lay;
It seemed as if the hour were one
Sent from beyond the skies,
Which scattered from above the sun
A light of Paradise.

Percy Bysshe Shelley

tommy the turtle

My husband and I had been living on the island of Maui for more than a year when we had an aha moment. Both of us worked from home and some days we never left the house. Here we were, within easy walking distance of some of the world's most beautiful beaches, yet the only time we gazed at one was when we looked at a family photo on our screen savers.

We decided—no, we declared—that every Tuesday and Thursday would be beach days. Period. End of discussion.

Except that my husband thought the best time to hit the sand would be four in the afternoon after most of the visitors had returned to their condos and hotel rooms with sunburnt shoulders.

Being a morning person, I campaigned for a nine o'clock arrival time. That would give us three hours in the water and in our beach chairs before the sun was at its zenith. Plus, we would be long gone before the afternoon winds kicked up whitecaps on the waves.

The next Tuesday we agreed to try out the four o'clock option. As predicted, the crowds had dispersed and only a dozen people remained on the beach. We set up our chairs and high-stepped into the water, with the wind sending sea spray into our faces. The waves were small but seemed to be curling in a lather close to the shore, where they clawed the sand and dragged it back to sea in fistfuls. That should have been our warning sign.

Eagerly, we pushed beyond the churned-up mess at the shoreline and swam out farther than usual, moving out of the silty water. Our plans to float and talk were cut short when we realized we were being pulled out by a strong undertow.

We knew enough to remain calm and swim parallel to the shore. In the pocket where the waves receded and the water swirled, we thought we could find an opening back to the beach.

I caught a rising swell and swam into the opening, where a large wave pushed me down face-first. The wave seemed to possess powerful fingers that were clenched into a fist, and I was being turned upside down and right side up. I surfaced and gasped for air before the watery fist curled again, and I was spun around like a tennis ball in a dryer. With a final saltwater shove, I was spit out on the shore.

Crawling away from the waves, I tried to catch my breath. My heart raced. I turned to see that my husband hadn't been pulled into the same opening that propelled me to safety. He was still far out in the water and had stopped swimming. He was waving both arms over his head. I realized he was yelling for help.

Before I could call out or pull myself up to go for help, I saw that one of the few people left on the beach was running to the water with his boogie board. I stumbled through the sand to where the young man entered. A woman joined me, asking if I was okay. I tried to answer but found I could only cough, dislodging the

Drifting

And now the sun in tinted splendor sank,
The west was all aglow with crimson light;
The bay seemed like a sheet of burnished gold,
Its waters glistened with such radiance bright...

Our boat was drifting slowly, gently round,
To rest secure till evening shadows fell;
No sound disturbed the stillness of the air,
Save the soft chiming of the vesper bell.

Olivia Ward Bush-Banks

sand caught in my throat. With my arms over my head, I waved frantically to my husband, who was drifting farther out. Could he see that help was on the way?

The rescuer paddled his board beyond the crunching waves. My husband kicked and stroked, trying to swim closer to him. The woman beside me put her arm around me. We waited and watched as the two men connected, and my husband gripped the board.

Together they held on, kicked vigorously, and caught a messy swell that pulled them forward. Another wave shot them up, then down, and with a tumble, both men fell onto the shore, panting.

It was a while before any of us spoke, except for hoarsely repeated thank-yous. When words came more easily, the experienced young man had firm words of caution for us. We received a lesson on currents and waves and how to read the water before entering.

"Never turn your back on *moana*. On the ocean," he said.

"Always respect *ke kai*. The sea," he added, covering all the bases.

We nodded. We understood. We will always remember what happened that day.

...the wide blue stillness
of the sleeping sea,
the swish of its quiet swell
making long, slow folds
in the silky water...

Hector Berlioz

For the next two weeks we silently disregarded our pact to go to the beach every Tuesday and Thursday. Then an especially gorgeous day dawned and *moana* beckoned us to return. This time, we arrived at my suggested morning hour and trekked down to the other end of the beach, which, we had been told, was a safer place to swim. We settled in our beach chairs, taking the time to study the curves of the shore breaks and admire how clear the water was.

A few locals already were splashing about, beyond where the waves crested. The water was clear and calm and once again looked like the Hawaiian waters we were used to swimming in. The welcome mat was out, and we entered the liquid turquoise while hiding our slight nervousness.

I went in the water first, diving under the oncoming wave and feeling the invigorating surge that always comes on that first immersion. Coming up on the other side, I heard my husband calling out to me. A surge of panic rose. But the fear immediately receded when I saw what he was pointing at.

I had come up from the wave close to a large turtle. His knobby head, the size of a pear, poked up only a few feet away from me. His shell was easy to view under the clear water and was the size of my favorite large salad bowl. His long back flippers were slowly pushing him away from where I bobbed. I'd seen many sea turtles at a distance at Ho'okipa Beach where they often came up onto the sand. From South Maui, I'd seen their heads pop up occasionally in the waters of the beaches of Makena and Keawakapu. But I'd never seen a turtle when I was in the water.

Even though I wanted to swim beside my new friend, and the fantasy lover in me longed to place my hand on his shell and be taken for a ride, I knew it was illegal to engage with any variety of endangered Hawaiian sea turtles by touching them or altering their natural behavior patterns. I also knew that sea turtles on Maui could live for eighty years. This guy could have been making this same swim every day long before I was born.

My husband caught up with where I was treading water. Together we watched the turtle swim away. A sense of serenity seemed to flow from the gentle creature's wake. His movements were so smooth and rhythmic.

I smiled at my favorite person in the world, and he smiled back at me.

In the years that followed, we endeavored to keep our beach dates on Tuesday and Thursday mornings. More than once we reminded each other that this was the same beach, the same waters, that could have taken our lives. Now it was our favorite beach, and these sun-kissed mornings were our favorites. I was glad we hadn't gotten so spooked that we gave up swimming in the sea.

Many Hawaiians have told me that the *honu*, the turtles, are sacred. I often thought of that on our date days because most mornings, right around 10:15, we would watch carefully for Tommy the Turtle, as we had named him. Almost always, our diligent pal came paddling along, carrying out his peaceful routine. His arrival always prompted me to thank our Creator for the extraordinary blessing of drinking in the beauty along with a sip of the terror of one of the most beautiful beaches in the world.

Come!

From an island of the sea
Sounds a voice that summons me,—
"Turn thy prow, sailor, come
  With the wind home!"

Sweet o'er the rainbow foam,
Sweet in the treetops, "Come,
Coral, cliff, and watery sand,
  Sea-wave to land!

"Droop not thy lids at night,
Furl not thy sails from flight!..."
Cease, cease, above the wave,
  Deep as the grave!

O, what voice of the salt sea
Calls me so insistently?
Echoes, echoes, night and day,—
"Come, come away!"

Walter de la Mare

breakfast on the beach

Morning became my favorite time of day during the decade my husband and I lived on Maui. I quickly developed a habit of going outside just before dawn. I would plant my feet on the tiny patch of grass in our backyard and draw in a deep breath, with my arms raised to the heavens. The earth nearly always felt warm, and the air was cool and fresh, laced with the scent of sweet tropical fruit and flowers.

I would set my face like an arrow toward the sliver of blue ocean that could be seen, if I stood in the right spot, just past the neighbor's royal palm. Here I lifted up what I called my "Prayers at First Light."

When I was young, I learned to initiate my conversation with our Heavenly Father before the wild rush of the day begins. Gratitude, adoration, and requests all tumbled out of my spirit as I stood in that sacred spot. I prayed with my eyes open, sipping in the view of the ocean and sky as if it were cool, sweet guava nectar meant to awaken my senses to the beauty and simple joys still left in this crumbling world.

One day an idea settled on me. I was thinking of the account in John 21 when Peter and six other disciples had been fishing all night and caught nothing. The risen Lord appeared on the shore and called out, asking if they had caught anything. Jesus told them to cast their net on the other side of the boat.

When they did, their net filled with fish, and John recognized the stranger on the shore as Christ. "It is the Lord!" he said.

Sometimes in my life I had nothing to show after much labor, and this passage would prompt me to cast my net on the other side, even if it didn't make sense. I longed to be like John and recognize when the voice of direction is the Lord's.

But the part that went deeper in me that morning was a simple observation: Jesus had breakfast on the beach with His friends.

When the disciples reached the shore with their treasure trove of fish, Jesus invited them to bring some of what they had. He was waiting for them, prepared for an intimate time with them. He already had a fire going with fish on the coals and bread.

That simple invitation to come, to be seen and known and included, always stirred something in me.

Instead of gazing at the beach at this glorious time of day, some days I could say to a friend, "Come." I could bring something to eat and initiate a valued conversation with her in the stillness of the new day. Such a gift was within my power to give to others.

I began my small sacred tradition of breakfast on the beach by telling a friend that I would come pick her up at 7:00 a.m. and return her home by 9:30. I didn't tell my friends where we were going, but I never had anyone turn down the mysterious invitation.

My hostess supplies hidden in the trunk included two low beach chairs, a low beach table, and an embroidered tablecloth I bought in Switzerland when I was twenty-one. I carefully packed my favorite china teapot, two china cups and saucers, English breakfast tea, cream in a small jelly jar, and a large thermos with hot water. Instead of fish, like Jesus served, I focused on the bread part of His menu with lovely croissants or muffins from a local bakery.

The maiden voyage of this new adventure was launched on a birthday girl who was both surprised and delighted when I parked at what, unbeknownst to me, was her favorite beach. We carried the gear to the sand and found we had the popular and typically crowded place to ourselves. The new day seemed to blush at our early arrival and sent its pink reflection across the glistening water.

We noted the island of Kahoolawe took on a rosy glow as the

sun warmed our backs. We sipped our tea and spread our mango jam on the croissants, our voices low and reverent. The waves seemed subdued and content to curl and uncurl without a lot of froth and thunder. Our hearts settled into the same contentment as we shared important details and landlocked feelings from our usual froth-and-thunder lives. Our conversation mattered.

We sighed and nodded, which were easy expressions of our affection for each other and our understanding of the confidential information we had shared. We were content to sit and stare at the glory all around us. The red cardinals that had been checking in seemed happy that we had shared some crumbs with them.

It seemed only right to conclude with a prayer for my friend. My heartfelt words tumbled over us as pristinely as the gentle waves washed across the shore. Together we welcomed a fresh new

day with no sorrow in it. Only hope and settled peace.

I knew then that this was something special. This unhurried, uninterrupted time was a chance to reset, to draw near, and to be restored. Doesn't that sound exactly like what Jesus did when He invited the disciples to bring what they had and to come, have breakfast on the beach?

I carried on the special tradition and toted my china teapot and accessories to the same remote beach many times. One friend and I discovered we share a love for cherry pie. I kidnapped her on her birthday morn, and she laughed when we settled in the sand and I lit a candle on a slice of cherry pie.

She surprised me with a return trip around my birthday and upped the fare with a scoop of ice cream that had not melted in her ice chest.

I will sing to the Lord as long as I live.
I will praise God to my last breath!
May he be pleased by all these thoughts about him,
for he is the source of all my joy.

Psalm 104:33-34 TLB

For one young woman, who was in a pocket of sorrow, we stopped to buy her favorite coffee on the way, and all I brought with the beach chairs were two party napkins, a container of her favorite cookies, and my Bible. I knew I didn't have the words of comfort she needed to hear. But the Psalms did.

As she burrowed her feet into the sand and sipped her coffee, she felt the freedom in our open-air privacy to let her tears fall. I read to her one psalm after another. No discussion was needed. Only the unsurpassed view, the ease of trusted friendship, and a morning shower of ancient, true, eternal words. The effects on her tattered soul were miraculous. On mine too.

Before we moved to the mainland, we had a huge garage sale. More than a dozen friends asked if I would put the low table out for sale. The compact table's accordion-like folding top and screw-on legs fit in a canvas bag that I could sling over my shoulder. I had used it with the friends who were asking if it was for sale.

I told them no. The table and the china teapot were going to California with me. It brought me to tears to think about leaving Maui, the home of my heart. I needed my table and teapot because they would help me dream of new friends and many more breakfasts on the beach.

Could It Be Today?

Gentle coo of mourning dove
First light comes to the land I love
Rosy clouds in matronly array
Gather sunbeams and awaken the day

A brimming cup of island sounds
Familiar scent of toasted ground
Island breeze through open door
Sunlight streaks on bamboo floor

Geckos scurry across the lanai
Hibiscus lift eager chins to the sky
Palm trees applaud with tattered fronds
Rich, new mercies faithfully dawn

Anticipation flutters, pauses and turns
In my soul deep longing burns
Creation, you are not alone.
I, too, await the Gardener's return.

RJG

notes

Quote from Bryan Waller Procter, page 13,
　English Poems and Other Small Poems (Chapman and Hall, 1851).

"Exultation Is the Going" by Emily Dickinson, 1859, page 19.

"Exiled" by Edna St. Vincent Millay, 1921, page 25.

"A Seaside Walk" by Elizabeth Barrett Browning, 1887, page 27.

Quote from Ralph Waldo Emerson, page 32,
　Ralph Waldo Emerson, "Considerations by the Way," *Self-Reliance and Other Essays*
　(Boston: James Munroe and Co., 1844).

Quote from E.E. Cummings, page 42,
　E.E. Cummings, "maggie and milly and molly and may," *95 Poems* (New York: Harcourt,
　Brace, 1958).

Quote from Lucy Maud Montgomery, page 45,
　Lucy Maud Montgomery, *Anne of Green Gables* (Boston: Page Company, 1908).

Quotes from Anne Morrow Lindbergh, pages 51 and 134,
　Anne Morrow Lindbergh, *Gift from the Sea* (New York: Random House, 1955).

"I Started Early" by Emily Dickinson, 1862, page 53.

Quote from Helen Keller, page 56,
　Helen Keller, *The Story of My Life* (New York: Doubleday, Page & Co., 1902).

"The Love of God Is Greater Far" by Frederick M. Lehman, 1917, page 57.

"It Is a Beauteous Evening" by William Wordsworth, 1807, page 61.

Poem by Alfred, Lord Tennyson, 1870, page 62.

"How Dear to Me the Hour" by Thomas Moore, 1841, page 65.

Quote from Herman Melville, page 70,
　Herman Melville, *Moby-Dick or The Whale* (New York: Harper and Brothers, 1981).

Quote from Lord Byron, page 71,
　Lord Byron, *The Works of Lord Byron* (London: John Murray, 1842).

Quote from Jack London, page 75,
　"The Psychology of the Surboard," *Mid-Pacific Magazine*, May 1915.

Quote from Vincent van Gogh, page 77,
　Vincent van Gogh, *The Complete Letters of Vincent Van Gogh* (The New York
　Graphic Society, 1958).

"The Secret of the Sea" by Henry Wadsworth Longfellow, 1850, page 80.

Quote from George Herbert, page 83,
>The Poetical Works of George Herbert and Reginald Heber (Gall and Inglis, 1860).

Quote from Henry Wadsworth Longfellow, page 86,
>Longfellow's Poetical Works (Henry Frowde, London, 1893).

"Echoes" by Walter de la Mare, 1930, page 94.

Quote from Jacques-Yves Cousteau, page 96,
>Jacques-Yves Cousteau, "At Home in the Sea", National Geographic 125, no.4 (April 1964).

Journal entries from Betsey Stockton, pages 100–105,
>Betsey Stockton's Hawaiian journal was published by Ashbel Green in his periodical The Christian Advocate, 1824 and 1825.

"Eternal Father, Strong to Save" by William Whiting, 1861, page 105.

"The Golden Hour" by Thomas Moore, 1884, page 107.

"Lines Composed in a Wood on a Windy Day" by Anne Brontë, 1846, page 112.

Quote from Victor Hugo, page 114,
>Victor Hugo, Les Misérables (Brussels: A. Lacroix, Verboeckhoven & Cie, 1862).

"A Touch of Paradise" by Robert Greenwald, page 122,
>This poem was written by a friend of the family who never had it published. Used with permission.

"A Day of Sunshine" by Henry Wadsworth Longfellow, 1871, page 129.

Quote from C.S. Lewis, page 139,
>C.S. Lewis, The Lion, the Witch and the Wardrobe (London: Geoffrey Bles, 1950).

"Address to the Ocean" by Bryan Waller Procter, 1887, page 141.

Quote from Don Blanding, page 147,
>Don Blanding, "Morning on the Beach," Paradise Loot (Honolulu: H. T. Patten, 1925).

"To Jane: The Recollections" by Percy Bysshe Shelley, 1839, page 155.

"Drifting" by Olivia Ward Bush-Banks, 1914, page 159.

Quote attributed to Hector Berlioz, thought to have been written in 1832, page 160.

"Come!" by Walter de la Mare, 1906, page 163.

photo credits

Cover © Daniel Gonzalez / Stocksy

Back cover © Justina Atlasito; Pong471 / Shutterstock

3 © Marzufello / Shutterstock

3, 42, 140, 153 © Zee''s Graphi Stock / Shutterstock

4 © Oveskyfly / Shutterstock

7, 112 © Willyam Bradberry / Shutterstock

8, 9 © Taylor Wilson Smith / Shutterstock

10 © Gung De Setiawan / Shutterstock

12 personal collection of Robin Jones Gunn

13, 35 © VolodymyrSanych / Shutterstock

14, 167 © jakkapan / Shutterstock

17, 43, 117, 122 © icemanphotos / Shutterstock

19, 87, 95, 116 © Viktoriia_Patapova / Shutterstock

20, 21 © Anton_Burkhan / Shutterstock

22 © Kittisun / Shutterstock

25, 27, 130 © Ben Mack / Pexels

28 © Tj LeClair / Shutterstock

31 © ameenfahmy / Unsplash

32 © A.I / Shutterstock

33, 40, 94, 125, 152 © Jess Loiterton / Pexels

36 © Davut ERDEM / Pexels

38 © Dmitry Molchanov / Shutterstock

44 © TravnikovStudio / Shutterstock

47 © Streamlight Studios / Shutterstock

48 © Olga Sömek / Pexels

50 © Karolina Kaboompics / Pexels

52, 132 © Norrapat Thepnarin / Shutterstock

53 © ArtHouse Studio / Pexels

54 © Alonzo Photo / Pexels

56 © Anastasia Shemetova / Shutterstock

57 © Linus Nylund / Unsplash

58 © Kizoa Team / Unsplash

61, 135 © elena moiseeva / Shutterstock

62 © Zaksheuskaya / Shutterstock

65 © xandtor / Unsplash

66, 67 © Dudarev Mikhail / Shutterstock

68 © barmalini / Shutterstock

70 © KORAGOT / Shutterstock

71 © OneyWhyStudio / Shutterstock

73 © Leonardo Gonzalez / Shutterstock

75, 96, 110 © chyworks / Shutterstock

76 © LuckyStep / Shutterstock

78 © Matt Jenssen / Pexels

80, 107, 133 © Taryn Elliott / Pexels

82 © Doni Haris / Pexels

84 © Nathan Cowley / Pexels

86 © Oksana_SR / Shutterstock

88, 89 © Panikhin Sergey / Shutterstock

90 © jsnover / Getty Images

93 © HereAndThere / Shutterstock

97 © Joshua Rainey Photography / Shutterstock

98 © Roberto Nickson / Unsplash

101 © Francesco Ungaro / Pexels

102, 103 © Unchalee Khun / Shutterstock

104 © Savion Wooley / Shutterstock

108 © Mani102 / Shutterstock

115 © Maxim Studio / Shutterstock

118, 119 © Iakov Kalinin / Shutterstock

120 © lucas_moore / Shutterstock

126 © De Visu / Shutterstock

129 © Mikbiz / Shutterstock

136 © SaintM Photos / Getty Images

138 © Delbars / Shutterstock

141 © Earth / Unsplash

142 © Drew Colins / Unsplash

145 © Anton Plutov / iStock

146 © Firman K / Shutterstock

148 © Coco Ratta / Shutterstock

150 © guille pozzi / Unsplash

155 © PrasitRodphan / Shutterstock

156 © Kammeran Gonzalez-Keola / Pexels

159 © JittiNarksompong / Shutterstock

160 © KanokpolTokumhnerd / Shutterstock

163 © Jake Houglum / Shutterstock

164 © Anastasiia Krivenok / Getty Images

168 © Vera NewSib / Shutterstock

171 © Olga Zarytska / Shutterstock

172 © Emily Shirron / Unsplash

Endsheet photos © antstang; icemanphotos; junaidslife;

       Delpixel / Shutterstock

Umbrella icon © Turac Novruzova / Getty Images

about the author

Robin Jones Gunn is the bestselling author of more than one hundred books, including the timeless Christy Miller series. Her multi-award-winning Christian fiction includes the Glenbrooke, Sisterchicks, and Suitcase Sisters series. Hallmark Channel created four Christmas movies inspired by her novels. Three network record-breaking movies were based on her Father Christmas novellas.

Robin's popular nonfiction includes *Victim of Grace* and *Praying for Your Future Husband*. She cohosts the *Women Worth Knowing* podcast and is a frequent speaker at international and local events.

Robin and her husband have two grown children and four grandchildren. They make their home in southern California and live by the sea.

Visit robingunn.com
@RobinGunn
@Robin Jones Gunn

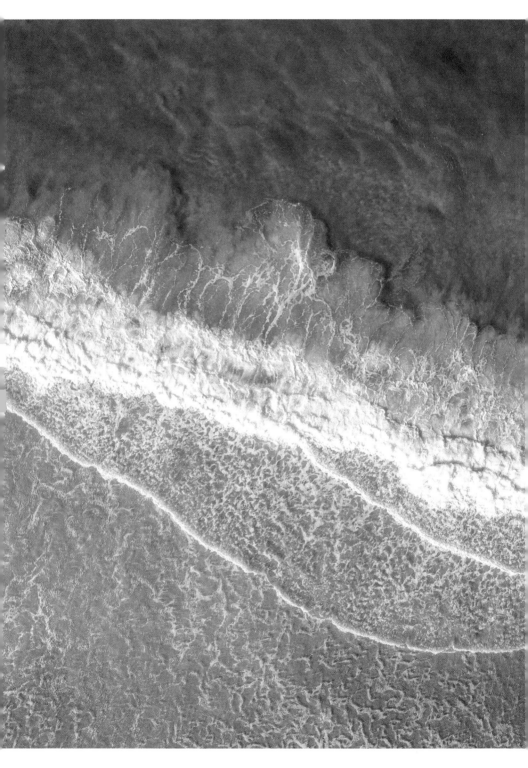